CONTENTS

INTRODUCTION 6	DAN GURNEY 86
JOHN SURTEES 8	MIKE HAILWOOD 94
TAZIO NUVOLARI 14	JACKIE STEWART 102
RUDOLF CARACCIOLA 22	MARIO ANDRETTI 110
BERND ROSEMEYER 30	NIKI LAUDA 118
HERMANN LANG 34	GILLES VILLENEUVE 126
ALBERTO ASCARI 38	DIDIER PIRONI 130
JUAN MANUEL FANGIO 46	ALAIN PROST 134
STIRLING MOSS 54	NIGEL MANSELL 142
JACK BRABHAM 62	AYRTON SENNA 150
JIM CLARK 70	AN UNSUNG HERO 158
GRAHAM HILL 78	PICTURE CREDITS 160

PIRELLI ALBUM OF MOTOR RACING HEROES

INTRODUCTION

This is not a book about individual acts of heroism. It is concerned with dedicated motor racing drivers whose ability and competitiveness has been outstanding amongst their contemporaries.

Although some of my twenty heroes were world champions, not all were among the most successful drivers. Some never had cars good enough to match their abilities. Others were carried away by the dream of creating their own racing machines. A few died before their full potential could be realised.

They vary considerably in personality and background. They differ in their behaviour off the track, in their relationships within the team, and in their approach to the grid.

Yet, despite the many differences, all my motor racing heroes have one thing in common—they went beyond mere flirtation with the dangers and challenges of racing. Each sustained a genuine passion to excel in the sport. In recent years, for example, I have had the opportunity to drive a 1937 Mercedes W125 and the 12-cylinder W154 on circuits such as Spa, Hockenheim and Silverstone. This experience has brought home to me the huge courage and skill of the drivers of that time.

The driver-car relationship is crucial. Each of these heroes was able to obtain the very best from his car. By seeking the best possible understanding of both his own limits and the character and performance of the individual machine, each has constantly striven to improve his driving skills.

Such highly-motivated sportsmen, who consistently compete to the full extent of their ability, are to my mind the real heroes of motor racing.

John Surtees

JOHN SURTEES

John Surtees with his 1957 BMW 507 and his ex-Georg Meier 1939 TT-winning supercharged BMW motorcycle. Motorcycle and sidecar racing has a special place in his heart, for Surtees had been taken to motorcycle races as a babe in arms, literally starting his career as a passenger in his father's racing combination.

JOHN SURTEES

John Surtees began his illustrious career on two wheels. He became motorcycle world champion no fewer than seven times (three 350 cc and four 500 cc world titles). Unlike others, though, Surtees also became Formula One World Champion and Can-Am Champion. He created Team Surtees, which competed successfully in F5000, Formula Two and Formula One. John Surtees is one of our very special heroes and we salute him.

ROBERT NEWMAN
& DEREK FORSYTH
CO-PRODUCERS

Above: Off the ground at Ballaugh Bridge, 500 cc Senior TT, Isle of Man. John Surtees rides the 4-cylinder, 500 cc of MV Agusta, for whom he raced almost exclusively from 1956 to 1960. Previously he had competed mainly on Vincents, Nortons, REGs and NSUs, continuing to race Nortons and NSUs up to the autumn of 1957.

Left: 1960, Silver City Trophy, Brands Hatch. Surtees' first year in motor racing, when he graduated swiftly to Formula One for Team Lotus and also rode to win the 350 cc and 500 cc world championships for MV Agusta. John Surtees (right), his father John Norman Surtees (left) and Colin Chapman (centre).

Right: 1964, Mexican Grand Prix, Mexico City. (Left to right) Dan Gurney (winner), John Surtees (second), Jim Clark, Graham Hill.

JOHN SURTEES

1964, German Grand Prix, Nürburgring. Hill (left) and Bandini (right) congratulate Surtees on his victory. That season he was to go on to win at Monza, and his placing in the Mexican GP gained him the championship. His record as being the only man to have won championships on two wheels and on four remains unbroken.

1964, Monaco Grand Prix. Surtees in his Ferrari 158. For some time Enzo Ferrari had been running the team at a distance and so had to rely upon information which was often suitably adapted to meet informants' personal objectives before being passed up the line.

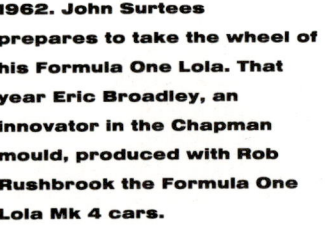

1962. John Surtees prepares to take the wheel of his Formula One Lola. That year Eric Broadley, an innovator in the Chapman mould, produced with Rob Rushbrook the Formula One Lola Mk 4 cars.

Left: 1966, Dutch Grand Prix, Zandvoort. Surtees in the Cooper-Maserati. That year, and the following, Cooper fitted a 3-litre V12 Maserati engine for the new Formula One. Surtees won the 1966 Mexican Grand Prix in one of these cars.

April 1972, Esso Uniflo Trophy, Thruxton. John Surtees in the TS10-Hart, Team Surtees' Formula Two car. This was Surtees' last racing year, though Team Surtees was to remain active until its last Grand Prix race six years later.

Left: John Surtees outside his home near Edenbridge, with his BMW 507. His interest in early racing heroes was kindled during the war years by his father's collection of motoring books and magazines, including back numbers of *Motor Cycle* and *Motorcycling* which featured the titans of the time.

PIRELLI
ALBUM OF MOTOR RACING
HEROES

JOHN SURTEES

with Sydney Higgins

D

DEALERFIELD

Many people have helped in bringing this book together. In particular we should like to acknowledge Rod Green, Anna Higgins, Jackie Hunt, Peter Ormiston, Adrian Sington, Jeremy Sykes and Isabella Villa.

Robert Newman & Derek Forsyth
Co-producers

First published in Great Britain in 1992 by
BOXTREE LIMITED
Broadwall House, 21 Broadwall
London SE1 9PL

This edition specially printed for Dealerfield Ltd – 1994

Pirelli Album of Motor Racing Heroes
Copyright © Pirelli Coordinamento Pneumatici SpA
and Derek Forsyth Partnership Limited 1992

Text Copyright © Team Surtees Ltd
and Syd Higgins Education Ltd 1992
Concept and co-producer Robert Newman
Art Director and co-producer Derek Forsyth
Designed by Derek Forsyth & Partners
Designer Gill White
Illustrator Jane Thomson
Historical Adviser Chris Nixon
Publishing Consultant Andrew Best

All rights reserved. No part of this publication may be reproduced, stored in a retrieval system, or transmitted, in any form or by any means, electronic, mechanical, photocopying, recording or otherwise, without the prior permission of the copyright holder.

A CIP catalogue record for this book is available from the British Library

ISBN 1 85927 049 2

THE HEROES

TAZIO NUVOLARI

Tazio Nuvolari made something of a career from beating opponents against the odds. His fighting spirit influenced Grand Prix racing for over a decade between the wars. His readiness to compete until the chequered flag came down, and to race regardless of injuries and ill-health, made him an Italian legend who is still revered to this day.

It was perhaps Nuvolari's dramatic win against tremendous odds in the 1935 German Grand Prix at the Nürburgring that secured his place in history. Driving for Scuderia Ferrari in a 330 bhp Alfa Romeo P3, he took on the combined might of the German Silver Arrows—the supercharged 430 bhp W25 Mercedes and the 375 bhp B-type Auto Unions—driven by masters such as von Brauchitsch, Caracciola, Stuck and Rosemeyer, amongst others. The race brought an astonishing victory for Nuvolari who, with the aid of a light drizzle, picked up something like 45 seconds on the last lap before fate took a hand and the leading Mercedes of von Brauchitsch blew a tyre at the Karussell turn.

Only 5 ft 3 in (1.6m) tall, this slender, wiry man started his career, as did I, racing motorcycles. Enzo Ferrari, against whom Nuvolari raced at first, and later joined, described him as abrupt, single-minded and hard to get to know. Ferrari recalled that Nuvolari admonished him for buying a return ticket for the Targa Florio—when you are going to a race you should always anticipate the possibility that you might not come back! I have heard many hair-raising stories of the

Right: Nuvolari began his racing career on motorcycles.

Targa Florio of that time, and indeed have competed in the race, so I can well understand Nuvolari's sentiment.

On motorcycles he had at first been famed for his daredevil style, but victories had come, especially after he joined Bianchi in 1925. Here, I am reminded of my own career in that he was offered the chance to drive for Alfa Romeo and so, as I did in the late fifties, would race

15

Nuvolari's famous talisman was a gold pin in the shape of a tortoise that he always wore at his neck when driving. It was presented to him by the poet Gabriele d'Annunzio and bore the legend *For the fastest man in the world, the slowest creature in the world.* Above is a replica.

Nuvolari in his racing gear—leather helmet, monogrammed yellow jersey, and tortoise-shaped pin.

Far right: 1930, Cuneo mountain climb. Nuvolari straddles the radiator of his Alfa Romeo, Enzo Ferrari on right.

bikes one week and cars the next. The story is told that while testing at the Monza circuit the gearbox seized on the car and he spun off the track. Badly knocked about, he was ordered to rest for at least a month. Ten days later, literally strapped into an approximate racing position by the doctors, he was lifted onto his bike for the Grand Prix des Nations motorcycle race, which he won.

Ferrari first met Nuvolari in competition at the 1924 Circuito del Savio. Ferrari was amazed at the 'skinny Nuvolari' as he described him, for while he finished first in his 3-litre Alfa, Nuvolari came second in a 1.5-litre Chiribiri.

Unshaken in his determination to race cars, even to the point of selling some family land in order to buy a type-35 Bugatti, eventually Nuvolari was invited to join Scuderia Ferrari in 1930 to drive the Alfas.

Over the next year he achieved an impressive string of successes. In particular, the Italian public responded to his passion for racing and his determination to win. The crowds adored him, for he was exciting to watch and Ferrari tells of his inimitable driving style.

Amongst others, Enzo Ferrari has given a written account of Nuvolari's technique on a bend. From what I can understand by reading between the lines, and from my own experience of driving some of the cars of the thirties, it seems that Nuvolari was one of the first genuinely to use the throttle to steer his car. An inbuilt characteristic of these cars was a natural understeer. Nuvolari would counteract this—as Enzo Ferrari describes it—by 'smashing his foot down on the gas' and keeping it flat on the floor, setting up a four-wheel drift at a corner which would leave him perfectly placed with power fully applied for the exit.

In the summer of 1933, Nuvolari created a sensation in Italy by announcing that he was leaving Alfa.

Nuvolari's racing helmet and glove, which are preserved in his Mantova museum

Left: 1936, Monza. Early testing with the 8-cylinder 3.8-litre Alfa Romeo. (L-R) Tadini, Brivio, Nuvolari, Pintacuda, Farina.

During the 1934 season, he raced both Bugatti and Maserati cars as an independent.

In April, during the Bordino Grand Prix at Alessandria, his Maserati crashed into Varzi's Alfa Romeo and was hurled down a steep bank. Nuvolari fractured a leg and sustained severe internal injuries. It was feared for some time that he wouldn't survive, but, a few weeks later, he drove at the AVUS track in Berlin with the pedals of his Maserati adapted so he need use only his left foot because his right leg was still in plaster. He finished fifth.

At the end of 1934, at the insistence of Mussolini, no less, Nuvolari rejoined Scuderia Ferrari. It was the dawn of the era that was to be dominated by the astonishing silver cars of Mercedes-Benz and Auto Union. The race above all others that they were expected to win for the Fatherland in 1935 was the German Grand Prix. Nuvolari had other ideas. In his outdated, underpowered Alfa Romeo, he battled for over four hours against the might of the Silver Arrows. On the final lap, he was lying second, some 30 seconds behind Manfred von Brauchitsch in his straight-eight-cylinder, 4.3-litre supercharged Mercedes W25. Midway round the final lap, the left rear tyre of the Mercedes exploded and Nuvolari swept past. A deafening shout erupted from the vast German crowd as *il Mantovano Volante* took the chequered flag to secure his most outstanding victory. So confident had the officials been of a German win that they hadn't provided a recording of the Italian national anthem. But it was played. Nuvolari had brought along a copy of

Above top: 1935, German Grand Prix, Nürburgring. A pit stop for Nuvolari and the Alfa in which he beat the combined might of the Silver Arrows. During that year Alfa Romeo would on occasion provide the only real opposition to the German cars.
Above: 1939, British Grand Prix, Donington. Nuvolari drives to victory for Auto Union.

Tazio Nuvolari towards the end of his life.

Far right: 3 September 1939, Yugoslav Grand Prix, Belgrade. Nuvolari driving the supercharged D-type 3-litre Auto Union to victory. This was the last race for Auto Union who, unlike Mercedes-Benz, did not resume racing after the Second World War.

In the 1947 Mille Miglia, Nuvolari drove an open 1500 cc Cisitalia. He was in the lead in torrential rain until ignition troubles forced him to slow down. He finished second to a 2.9-litre Alfa driven by Biondetti who commented, 'I didn't win. I merely finished first.'

Nuvolari attends the 1952 Modena Grand Prix about a year before his death.

his own just in case there should be a need for it!

His famous victories and remarkable escapes continued. At Tripoli in 1936, he was thrown out of his Alfa and broke several ribs. The next day, encased in plaster, he took part in the Grand Prix and finished seventh. At Turin in April 1937 his car skidded, hit a tree, overturned and pinned him underneath. Early in 1938, during practice at Pau, his new Alfa caught fire and he managed to escape with only minor burns. Nevertheless, Nuvolari was angered by the potentially fatal incident at Pau, which suggested to him that he had been given an unsafe car. So he vowed he would never again drive an Alfa Romeo. Then, in the summer of that same year, came the shocking news of Rosemeyer's death on a stretch of German *autobahn*. This suddenly opened a place in the Auto Union team, and Nuvolari was very quick to seize the opportunity.

I can well imagine how he felt, after my all too brief drive in a V12, 485 bhp D-type Auto Union at Silverstone in 1990. It is a difficult car. But Nuvolari swiftly adapted his driving technique, winning two championship races during that same season, and in 1939 winning—in Yugoslavia—the last Grand Prix before war brought all racing to a halt.

The war over, Ferrari announced the first car to bear his name, and recorded that in 1947 Nuvolari telephoned him. 'Ferrari,' he said, 'I am ready to go.' Ferrari also recorded the Mille Miglia of 1948, the last experience that they shared together, when the 55-year old Nuvolari astonished everyone by his performance. He should have won, but a pivot pin in the suspension broke. 'Don't worry,' Ferrari commented, 'we shall win next year.' 'At our age there aren't many days like this left,' Nuvolari replied.

That same year, Nuvolari retired from racing, his lungs destroyed by the toxic fuels of those times. After a long illness he died on 11 August 1953. In a procession over a mile long, 25,000 people followed his coffin through the streets of Mantova. As he had requested, he was buried in his famous racing gear—a yellow jersey to which was pinned the ever-present gold tortoise, light blue trousers and his leather wind helmet.

TAZIO NUVOLARI

RUDOLF CARACCIOLA

Rudolf Caracciola without doubt had a special place in the hearts of racing enthusiasts. His ability was extraordinary and his performances were consistently outstanding. After a serious accident in 1933, he was told he would never be able to race again. In little over a year, however, he returned triumphantly to Grand Prix racing.

1931, German Grand Prix, AVUS. Caracciola in the SSKL Mercedes in which he scored one of his six German Grand Prix victories.

In 1964, I made a return visit to the Nürburgring after winning my first Formula One and sports car races there the previous year. I had just won my second successive German Grand Prix, and on 2 August I had the good fortune to meet Alice Caracciola, Caracciola's widow. We discussed her husband Rudi's driving experience and his attitude to and thoughts about the Ring. We also talked about our mutual love for her home town, Lugano, just over the border from where I had been based with MV Agusta.

Alice was the second of Caracciola's wives, both of whom had been wonderfully supportive throughout his career and particularly so during the times that he suffered major injuries.

Except for one brief spell with Alfa Romeo when at first, to satisfy the Italian drivers, his car was painted white to distinguish it from the Italians' racing red, Caracciola drove entirely for Mercedes-Benz for, while of Italian origin, he was in fact a typically elegant and formal German. It was, therefore, with some reluctance that Enzo Ferrari, from first-hand knowledge of his performance, admitted that he could probably be considered one of the best drivers of all time.

Caracciola started motor racing in 1922 at the age of 21 while working as a car salesman. In 1926, the first ever German Grand Prix was held at the famous AVUS track in Berlin. Driving a privately-entered Mercedes-Benz, Caracciola stalled at the start. By the time his mechanics succeeded in push-starting the car, Caracciola was over a minute behind the rest of the field. Then it started to rain, and so his reputation of 'Rainmaster' was born. Caracciola, the reports say, drove superbly in

Hans Stuck, Charly and Rudi Caracciola, on a skiing holiday in the early 1930s. Rudi had won the first ever German Grand Prix in 1926 in heavy rain, and so was dubbed 'Rainmaster'. He and Charly were married shortly afterwards.

Left: April 1933, Monaco. Caracciola being carried away after crashing his Alfa Romeo in practice. The Monte Carlo doctors were to say that he would never race again.

1934, French Grand Prix, Montlhéry. This marked Caracciola's return to Grand Prix racing—in the W25 Mercedes—after his fearful crash in practice at Monaco the previous year. Charly had died while skiing only a few months earlier.

Enzo Ferrari recalled a race at Pescara in 1932, which was won by Nuvolari with Caracciola just 15 seconds behind him. Caracciola protested at being kept in the pits so long for refuelling. In fact, his car was running on German tyres specially prepared for Pescara's long straights. However, the circuit had mysteriously sprouted a couple of chicanes which reduced the internal heat generated by the tyres, so Nuvolari was able to use the new softer compound Pirelli Super-sport tyres to advantage.

appalling conditions. He won not only the race but a substantial sum in prize money, sufficient to enable him both to marry his girlfriend, Charly, and to open a Mercedes showroom in Berlin.

While his racing career prospered, the world's economy faltered. After the 1929 Wall Street Crash had forced him to close his business, he and Charly decided to move to Arosa, in Switzerland. At the end of 1930, the Depression forced Mercedes-Benz out of racing, but the company continued to give Caracciola customer support during 1931, which proved to be an extremely successful year for him. His 11 victories included the Mille Miglia, the first time a non-Italian had ever won the classic road race.

Mercedes, still suffering from the slump, advised him that he could expect no support from them for 1932. Simultaneously, Aldo Giovannini, the Alfa team manager, in the teeth of opposition from the rest of his team—Nuvolari, Borzacchini and Campari—offered Caracciola a contract which he accepted.

The 1932 season brought some successes and some near misses. He almost won the Mille Miglia again, but his car dropped a valve. Uncharacteristically, he held back at Monaco and let Nuvolari win. But he won the German Grand Prix, this time called the Eifel, for the fourth time, and the Monza GP. He also became European mountain champion by winning no fewer than five events. Then Alfa Romeo announced its

1934, French Grand Prix, Montlhéry. Caracciola shoots past the grandstands.

1937, Lugano. Rudi and Alice immediately after their marriage.

Far right: 1937, Monaco Grand Prix. Manfred von Brauchitsch leading Caracciola during their classic battle in this race. Von Brauchitsch won in defiance of Mercedes team orders.

withdrawal from racing, and Caracciola was again left high and dry.

Together with his great friend Louis Chiron, Caracciola formed a new team, Scuderia CC. But it was to be a short-lived partnership. In April 1933 at Monaco, after setting the fastest lap with Chiron the day before, Caracciola's front brakes locked. His Alfa, held to the right-hand side of the road, hit a stone wall. His right thigh was shattered, and the doctors at Monte Carlo Hospital told Charly that he would never race again—words that were to haunt me some thirty years later right after my own crash in Canada.

The surgeons wanted to operate, but Caracciola refused. Aldo Giovannini came to the rescue, and saw to it that he was taken to the Rizzoli Orthopaedic Institute in Bologna, a clinic still famous, particularly in motorcycle racing circles, for repairing the human chassis. About six months later he and Charly returned home to Lugano for his convalescence. His old friend Alfred Neubauer paid him a visit to announce that Mercedes were building a new 705 kg Formula car. Would he be fit to race? I cannot imagine a better spur to his recovery and, of course, there was only one answer.

Charly was coaxing him towards fitness. In January 1934 he signed his contract with Mercedes. Then tragedy struck. While skiing with friends, Charly was

Left: 1938, Swiss Grand Prix, Bern. Some key members of the Mercedes team. (Left to right) Rudolf Ulenhaut (technical director), Manfred von Brauchitsch (third), Rudolf Caracciola (winner), Dick Seaman (second), Max Sailer (a director of Mercedes-Benz), Alfred Neubauer (Mercedes team manager). It was Neubauer who invited Rudi to join the team once he had recovered from his accident at Monaco in 1933.

buried in an avalanche and died of a heart attack.

The 1934 season saw Caracciola make his comeback. All his old ability and fight were there, but it brought few successes. However, it was a different story in 1935. Sporting a pronounced limp but with all his strength recovered, he won six Grands Prix and became European champion. In this second spring of his career, he married Alice 'Baby' Hoffman, who had supported him so splendidly after Charly's death. That same year, 1937, driving a fabulous 5.6-litre W125 Mercedes, he regained the European championship, the title he had lost to Bernd Rosemeyer the previous year.

In 1938 he confirmed his superiority by winning the title yet again. The 1939 season—he was then 38 years old—did not go so well. He made a number of mistakes, and I believe that these can be accounted for by the fact that cars were changing considerably. At his age it must have been hard to adapt to the vast differences between the 125 and the new 154. Yet he won the German Grand Prix for the sixth time.

War broke out, and with it the golden age of Grand Prix racing came to an abrupt end. He and Alice continued to live in Lugano. The final chapter is a sad one. In 1946, aged 45, Caracciola went to America and drove at Indianapolis. He crashed in practice at high speed and sustained severe head injuries. With Alice's help he recovered, but slowly, and he still longed to race. Driving the exciting 300SL he finished fourth in the 1952 Mille Miglia. Then, in a similar car, he hit a tree during a race at Bern and smashed his left thigh. Finally, his career was over. He died in 1959 at the age of 58, with 15 Grands Prix and three European championships to his credit. Alice, the charming lady I'd met at the Nürburgring, lived on until the mid-seventies.

Above top: 1938, Coppa Acerbo, Pescara. Caracciola winning the race and his third European championship. Above: 16 September 1951, Monza. Caracciola with Jules Kötner of ADAC, the German motoring organisation.

BERND ROSEMEYER

Superb driving skills brought Bernd Rosemeyer a brief but spectacular Grand Prix career. From 1935 to 1937, he electrified spectators with his mastery of the enormously powerful, advanced but difficult mid-engined 16-cylinder Auto Union cars.

I have always said that if a motorcyclist is to change to cars the one thing he must show right from the start is speed. Technique and safety will come with experience. Bernd Rosemeyer was a prime example. Graduating from grass tracks to road racing, at the age of 23 he won six events for the NSU team, and was immediately signed for 1934 by the DKW motorcycle section of Auto Union, the year of Auto Union's successful debut in Grand Prix racing. At the end of the season, badly needing more top-class drivers, Auto Union invited 12 men, including Rosemeyer, to take part in driving trials. He was one of two selected to join Achille Varzi and Hans Stuck in the Auto Union team.

In his second race, the Eifel Grand Prix at the Nürburgring, he finished a close second to Rudolf Caracciola. He did even better in the season's last event at Brno in Czechoslovakia—he won. This meant that his first ever victory in a motor race was in a Grand Prix.

Rosemeyer and Auto Union dominated the 1936 season. They outclassed all opposition. Rosemeyer won five Grands Prix including the all-important German GP witnessed by an ecstatic crowd of 400,000 people. Rosemeyer became European champion. 1937 saw Caracciola and the Mercedes W125s turn the tables, but Rosemeyer achieved a famous victory in England at

Far Left: 1934. Rosemeyer racing for DKW.
Left: 1930. Rosemeyer with an RT100 motorcycle at his first grass track race.
Above: Bernd Rosemeyer with his wife, Elly Beinhorn, the famous German aviator.

1937, British Grand Prix, Donington. Rosemeyer bounds from the track in his 16-cylinder Auto Union.

Far right: 1936, German Grand Prix, Nürburgring. Wearing the victor's laurels, Rosemeyer is pushed by his mechanics towards the presentation dais.

1937, British Grand Prix, Donington. Rosemeyer in the pits after winning at Donington. This was his tenth and last Grand Prix and his last victory. Three months later he was killed.

the Donington Grand Prix. Tragically, it was to be his last. Three months later he was killed.

Spurred on by Hitler's desire to prove to the world the superiority of German mechanical and engineering expertise, the two state-subsidized car companies, Mercedes-Benz and Auto Union, became embroiled in fierce competition to establish clusters of speed records on stretches of *autobahn*.

On the freezing cold morning of 28 January 1938, just south of Frankfurt, Rosemeyer set off in an attempt to recapture his Flying Kilometre record which had been broken earlier that morning by Caracciola in his Mercedes. After nine kilometres, the Auto Union was swept out of control by a sudden crosswind. It crashed and disintegrated. Rosemeyer's body was found lying at the foot of some roadside trees.

Germany was shocked by the death of the young, extraordinarily gifted driver. Blond, handsome and carefree, he had in only three seasons achieved a reputation that few drivers could match.

HERMANN LANG

Hermann Lang's racing career started with motorcycle sidecar combinations. He was the 1931 German hillclimb champion. As a Grand Prix driver of the magnificent Silver Arrows which dominated motor racing in the late thirties, he became, in 1939, the team's most successful driver and European champion.

Far right: 1935, Eifel Grand Prix, Nürburgring. This was Lang's first race for Mercedes. He finished fifth.

After a spell of unemployment in 1932, Lang joined the Mercedes-Benz Experimental Department as an engine fitter, and worked on the new racing cars which were being prepared for the 1934 season.

When the cars were ready, he was made foreman mechanic to Luigi Fagioli, the Italian who was one of the three Grand Prix drivers in the Mercedes team. Lang, who would dearly have liked to race himself, had to be content with driving the cars to the starting grid or round the course for a few laps to bed-in new brakes.

At the end of the season, however, Alfred Neubauer, the formidable team manager of Mercedes, asked Lang to take part in some driver trials. Two experienced racing drivers also participated, but it was Lang, the motor mechanic, who was invited to join the Mercedes team as a reserve. In 1935 he had four Grand Prix drives. Not a great deal was expected of him and he performed only moderately well. But as he raced his confidence and driving skills developed.

Still only the reserve, he had a couple of outings during the 1936 season, but when it ended he was given a contract to become one of the team drivers for 1937.

Naturally, he was delighted. His senior team-mates, Rudolf Caracciola and Manfred von Brauchitsch, were less so. They reflected the then universally accepted

Above top: 1939, Eifel Grand Prix, Nürburgring. Lang in the Mercedes W163 on his way to victory.
Above: 13 August 1950, Solitude. Hermann Lang (right) makes a point in conversation with Paul Pietsch, while Manfred von Brauchitsch looks on.

34

HERMANN LANG

Left: 1950, Swiss Grand Prix, Bern. Hermann Lang in the pits.

May 1951, Spa. Off duty and in a lounge suit, German hero Hermann Lang settles into the cockpit of an Alfa 159.

Far right: 1952, Nürburgring. Hermann Lang with his wife Lydia.

Even though these three pictures were taken shortly after the war, they convey something of the flavour of pre-war motor racing. Note the worn timber stanchion at the old Nürburgring. John Surtees remembers his first visit to the Nürburgring in 1955: 'I began to absorb the unique history that surrounded the original circuit. The old hotel, with the ring of garages close by, lay tucked behind the great timber grandstands that fronted the pits, and the photographs and memorabilia on its walls vividly revived my childhood memories.'

image of a Grand Prix driver as coming from a well-to-do, even aristocratic, background. A mechanic from a working-class family was not expected to join such a glamorous elite. And, after all, Lang's racing experience had been restricted to a few gentle runs (not exceeding 3000 rpm) to bed-in brakes. Yet on one occasion when he did exceed this limit and drove at more than 120 mph for the first time in his life, chief mechanic Jakob Krauss turned a blind eye, perhaps sensing Lang's determination to become a racing driver.

The first race of the new season was in Tripoli. Lang won but, afterwards, he and his wife were so embarrassed at not having suitable evening clothes that they locked themselves in their hotel bedroom rather than go to the prize-giving. It was only when Neubauer insistently hammered on their door that they agreed to attend the glittering reception.

More victories followed, but they didn't come easily. Despite his constantly improving skills, Lang was still the junior driver in the team. This meant he sometimes had to submit to orders from Neubauer not to overtake the team's senior driver.

Despite this, Lang won the first three Grands Prix of 1939. Later in the season, by going against team orders and refusing to allow Caracciola to overtake him, he won the Swiss Grand Prix and became the 1939 European champion—the title that Caracciola had held in 1935, 1937 and 1938.

37

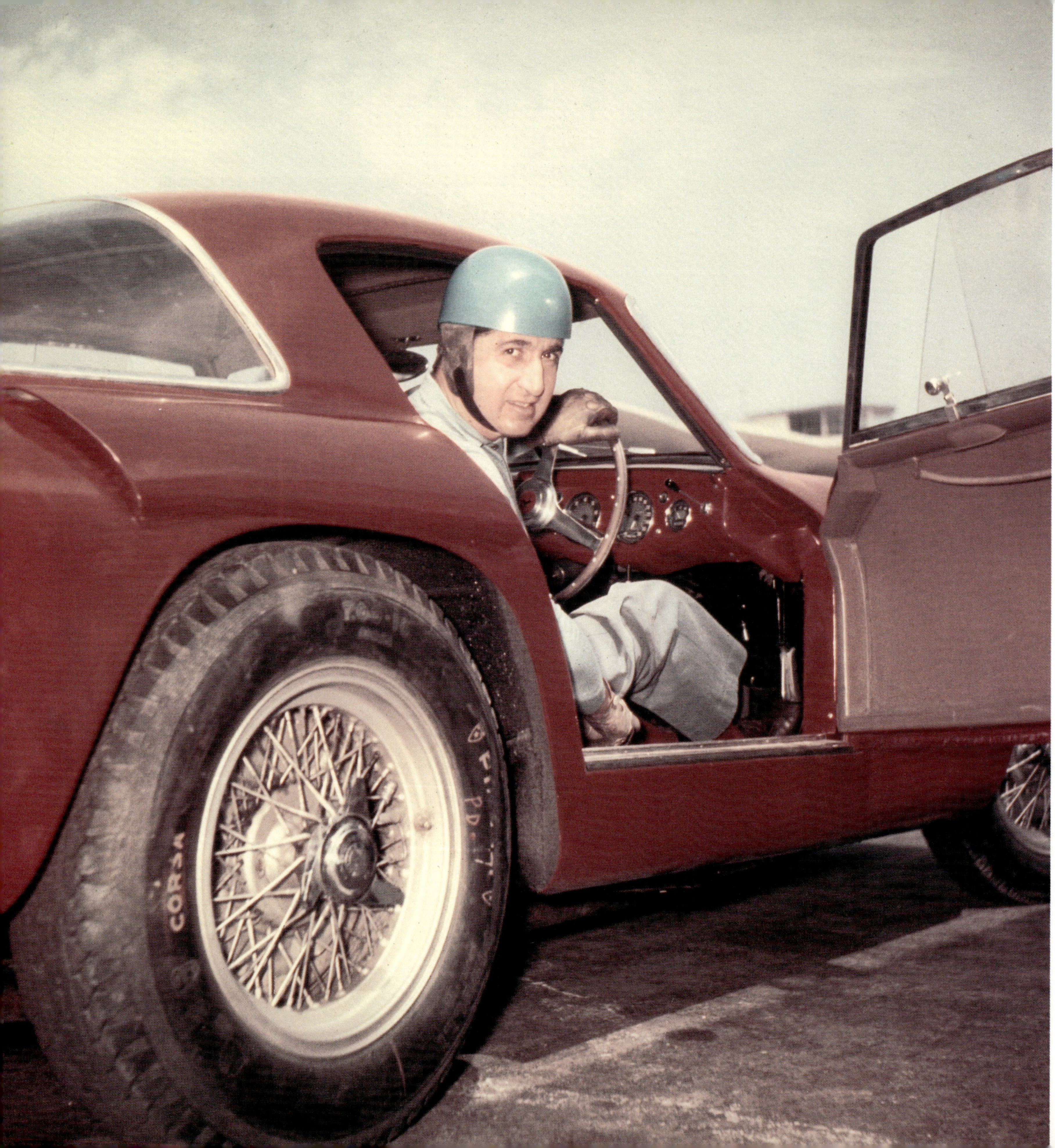
CORSA

ALBERTO ASCARI

Powerfully-built and one who took training for physical fitness seriously, Alberto Ascari was a strong-willed and talented driver. In 1955, during the Monaco Grand Prix, his Lancia D50 flew off the road and plunged into the harbour. He survived virtually unscathed. Four days later he was killed in a mysterious accident.

Ascari is another name which brings a twinkle to the eye of an Italian enthusiast. In the decade after the First World War, his father, Antonio Ascari, was one of the great Italian drivers. On 26 July 1925, he died after an inexplicable accident during the French Grand Prix at Montlhéry. He was 36.

At the time, Alberto was only six years old. He was 17 when he started his own racing career on motorcycles. During the next four years, he competed in many races on Sertum, Gilera and Bianchi bikes. His first car race was in 1940, when he drove Enzo Ferrari's first car, the Tipo 815, in the Mille Miglia, which that year was held over nine laps of a triangular 165 km (103-mile) course running from Brescia to Cremona and back.

The war brought his racing to an abrupt end. Nevertheless, encouraged by the veteran Italian driver, Luigi Villoresi, Ascari resumed his racing career in 1947. After a couple of years driving private Maseratis, he joined his friend and mentor, Villoresi, at Scuderia Ferrari in 1949. Already a precise and decisive driver who, according to Ferrari, was happiest as the hare but a reluctant hound, he was instantly successful.

Above: 1951, Italian Grand Prix, Monza. Alberto Ascari just before the start.
Left: 1924, French Grand Prix, Lyons. Antonio Ascari, Alberto's father, in his Alfa Romeo being push-started by his mechanic after a pit-stop.

The 1950 season saw the birth of the Formula One Drivers' World Championship. Giuseppe Farina and Juan Manuel Fangio in their Alfas dominated that year but, in 1951, Ascari, with two Grand Prix victories, was runner-up to Fangio.

3 September 1950, Monza. Enzo Ferrari in jovial mood.

1952, Italian Grand Prix, Monza. Ascari leading in his Ferrari during the season of his first world championship. This year and the next Formula Two rules applied and Ferrari was dominant.

Then the sport's governing body changed the rules. There were simply not enough Formula One cars. Alfa Romeo had withdrawn and BRM could not compete. In 1952 and 1953, therefore, the world championship was run according to Formula Two rules, with engines restricted to 2000 cc for unsupercharged cars or 500 cc for supercharged.

Fangio moved to Maserati, and Ferrari all but swept the board, creating a still unbroken team record of 14 successive Grand Prix wins. In both 1952 and 1953, Ascari was world champion and his own record of nine successive GP wins also remains unbroken.

For 1954 the championship reverted to Formula One, with enlarged limits of 2500 cc for unsupercharged engines and 750 cc for supercharged. With this change, Ferrari's dominance was broken. Ascari moved from Ferrari to Lancia. Fangio joined the new Mercedes-Benz team which, for the two years it raced, was all but invincible.

Lancia had a long way to go. Its new D50 Grand Prix car wasn't ready until the last race in 1954 and Ascari, the previous year's world champion, finished the season without a single championship point. A rare but significant success for him in a disastrous year was his victory in the Mille Miglia in the works Lancia D24.

It looked as though 1955 was going to be better. The first European Grand Prix of the season was at Monte Carlo. At half-distance Ascari had only to pass

The bag in which Alberto Ascari carried his racing gear. In these years races were frequent and a driver would expect to race 40 to 50 times a year. This travelling bag was Ascari's constant companion.

1950 saw the birth of the Formula One Drivers' World Championship. Farina and Fangio in their Alfas dominated that year but, in 1951, Ascari, with two Grand Prix victories, was runner-up to Fangio.

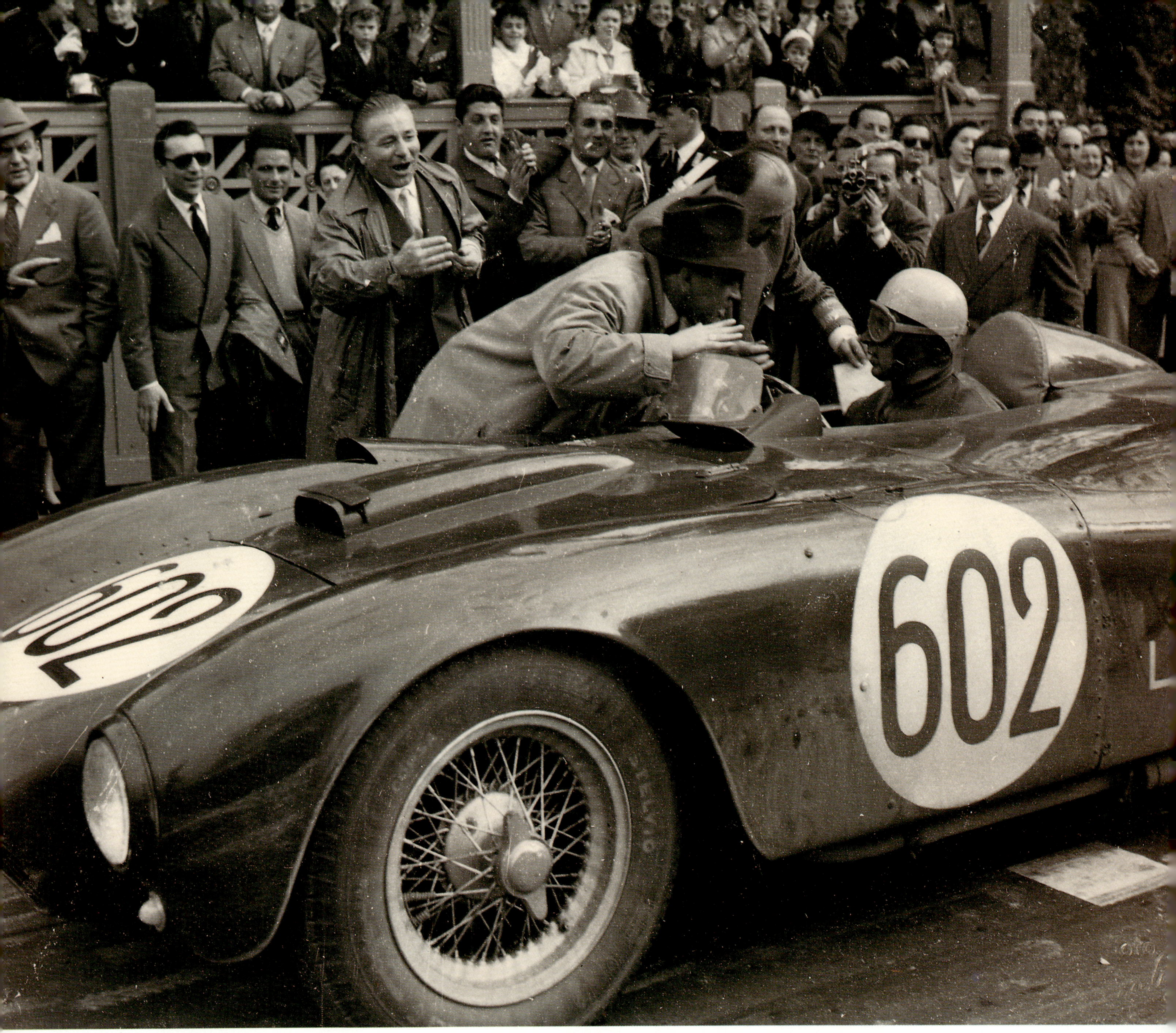
602

ALBERTO ASCARI

Left: 1954, Mille Miglia. Ascari at Mantova during his victorious drive in the Lancia D24.

3 September 1950, Monza Grand Prix. Ascari with Enzo Ferrari during practice.

1952, Italian Grand Prix, Modena. Ascari just before the start.

Stirling Moss in his stricken Mercedes to take the lead, but somehow he clipped the kerb at the chicane and plunged into the harbour. The Lancia disappeared into the sea in a cloud of spray and steam.

Happily, to the relief of the vast crowd of spectators, Ascari, still in his blue helmet, bobbed to the surface and swam to a rescue boat. He was taken to hospital where he was found to be suffering from no more than a broken nose. The doctors advised him to take a few days rest.

The following day, he returned to Italy, determined to take part in a 1,000 km sports car race at Monza the next weekend. Four days after the crash, on Thursday 26 May, Ascari, wearing a suit and tie, arrived at the Monza autodrome to watch Eugenio Castellotti, his co-driver, practice their 750S Ferrari.

After Castellotti had returned to the pits, Ascari unexpectedly decided to take the car out for a few laps during the team's lunch break. 'Don't worry,' he said, 'I'll drive slowly.'

Ascari was a superstitious man who regarded his light blue crash helmet as a lucky charm, so everybody there, including his old friend Villoresi, was amazed to see him put on Castellotti's white helmet.

43

7 September 1952, Italian Grand Prix, Monza. A cheerful Ascari on the starting grid.

Alberto Ascari (centre) with Nino Farina (left) and 'Gigi' Villoresi (right) — the Ferrari team.

Far right: 1955, Monaco Grand Prix. Ascari in his Lancia D50 leads team-mate Castellotti uphill towards the Casino. Tragically this was his last race.

He drove one lap slowly. On the second, he forgot his promise and clocked within a few seconds of Castellotti's fastest time that morning. On the third lap, the Ferrari swerved and left the ground. As it overturned, Ascari was flung out.

Villoresi was the first to reach the scene. Ascari was unconscious and died a few minutes later.

As Ascari was obsessed by lucky and unlucky numbers, much was made in the Italian press of the coincidences between his death and that of his father. Both died when they were 36, on the 26th day of a month, in an unexplained accident that took place four days after a miraculous escape.

Alberto Ascari's death shocked the motor racing world; in Italy, it was considered a national disaster. This typically Italian, thick-set racing driver was renowned for being a tough and stubborn competitor who was at his best when leading from the flag. Away from the track, he was mild-mannered and devoted to his wife and two children. He had won a special place in Italian hearts.

His body lay in state at Monza Hospital, his hands still wearing their racing gloves. On the day of his funeral, thousands of silent people lined the streets of Milan as the cortege passed slowly by. He was buried next to his father, who had died thirty years earlier.

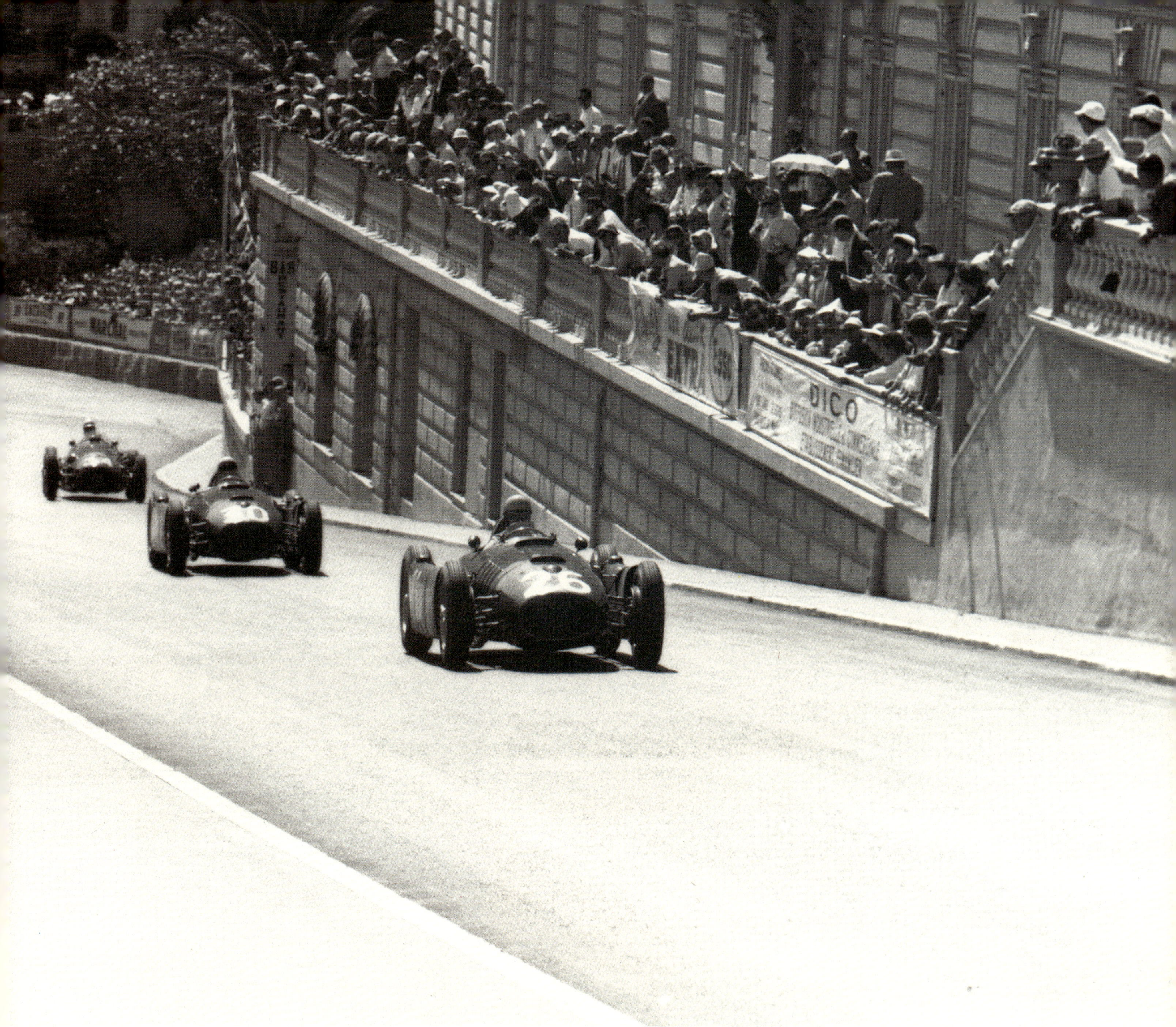
BAR
EXTRA
ESSO
DICO

JUAN MANUEL FANGIO

What is most astonishing about the great Fangio's Grand Prix career is not his success but that it happened at all. Coming from a rural backwater of Argentina, Juan Manuel Fangio was in his late thirties before he started his record-breaking conquest of a sport considered to be the preserve of European drivers and constructors.

Right: 1951, Monza. Fangio in the pits about to take his Alfa Romeo out on test.

Far right: 1957 Sebring. Fangio relaxes during an evening out with an unidentified partner.

As a driver, Fangio had exceptional skills, a high degree of confidence, great competitive intelligence, and an astonishing sense of balance—all of which brought consistent success. In his 51 world championship races, he started in pole position in 29 and won 24. He was world champion a record five times—in 1951 and from 1954 to 1957. Remarkably, his last title was won when he was 46 years old.

Stirling Moss has always said that Fangio was the greatest driver he ever raced against. Because I know how good Stirling was, his opinion confirms just how great a driver was Fangio.

As multiple world champion, Fangio was scrupulous in shouldering his responsibilities to his team and to his sport. Fluent in Spanish and Italian, he appeared to many to be a man of few words. Certainly he was happy to let others do the talking for him and refused to become embroiled in the machinations and politics that are all too prevalent in motor racing.

Blessed with a warm personality and an even temperament, he had a charismatic presence which inspired everyone around him, mechanics and fellow-drivers alike. After his retirement, he continued to be a notable ambassador for his sport and for his country.

In motor racing, Fangio is unique in being universally loved and respected. I've never heard a bad word said about him. His whole career exemplifies for me the difference between a good driver and a great driver. A good driver experiences the pace of the track with its competing cars as happening at speed. The truly great driver detaches himself from the speed factor and so

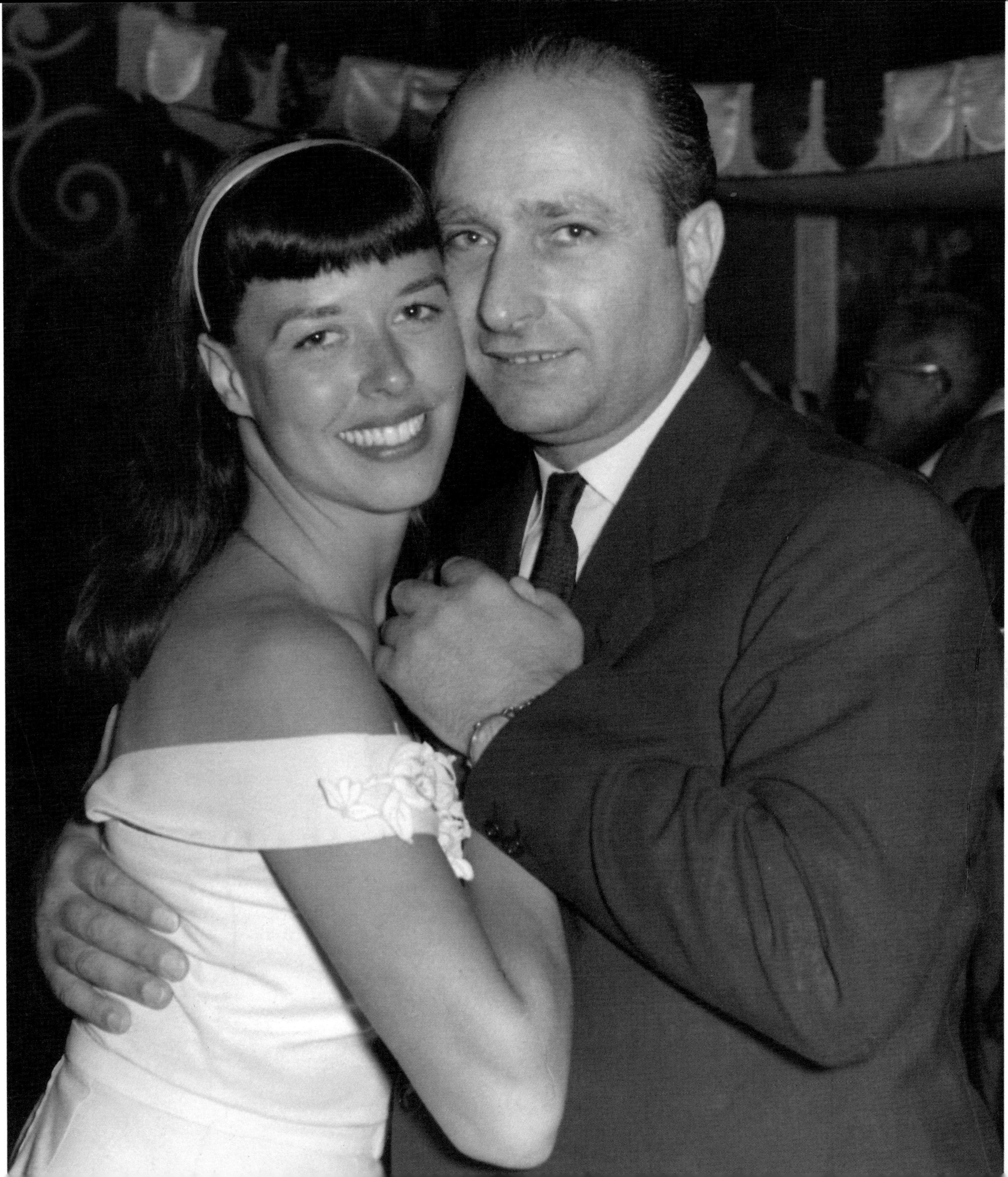

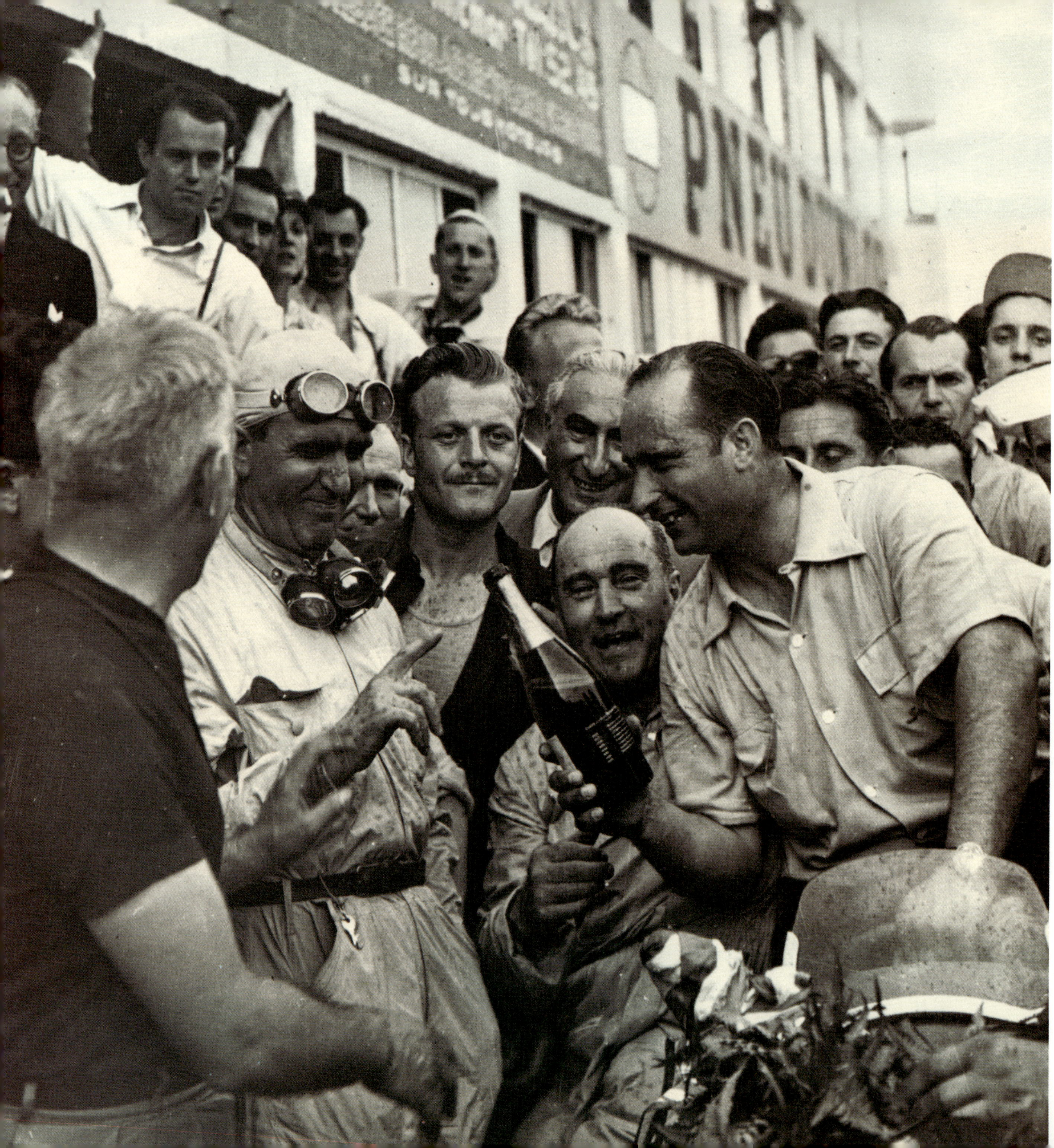

Left: 1950, French Grand Prix, Reims. Fangio after his win for Alfa Romeo celebrates with Nino Farina (wearing goggles) and (by his right shoulder) Luigi Fagioli.

1955, Belgian Grand Prix, Spa. Fangio on the road to victory in the Mercedes W196.

Right: 1952. Fangio in plaster after crashing his Maserati at Monza in June, cracking several vertebrae in his neck.

gains the mental room in which to perform with enhanced elegance and precision. By gaining time in his mind, he wins time in the race. This has remained Fangio's style in his retirement, unlike the many who remain caught up in the speed and hubbub of life.

Juan Manuel Fangio was born in 1911 in Balcarce, a small agricultural town south of Buenos Aires. He became a car mechanic and in 1932 opened his own workshop. In 1936, he made his driving debut in a borrowed taxi he'd specially modified for the race! Over the next decade, his career flourished in many long-distance races over the dirt roads of South America.

In 1948, he was sent to Europe by the Automobile Club of Argentina—ACA—as a member of its fact-finding mission to investigate the resurgent motor racing scene. After a couple of drives, he returned home.

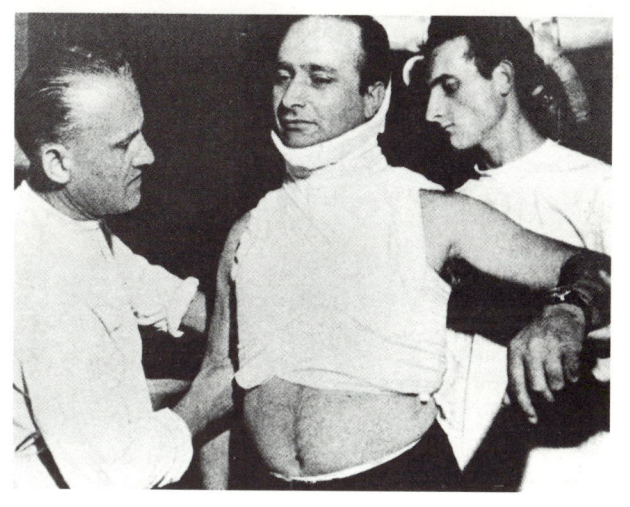

He was back again the following season. He won several minor French races in a Maserati and then, with a Ferrari Tipo 166 F2 bought by the ACA, he had an incredible victory in the Monza Grand Prix. On his return he found himself a national hero.

His win at Monza also impressed Alfa Romeo, who signed Fangio for the 1950 Formula One races

49

Fangio dominated Grand Prix racing from 1954 to 1957, winning the world championship in each of those years with many memorable victories.

1953, French Grand Prix, Reims. Mike Hawthorn in his Ferrari and Fangio in the Maserati. Neck and neck at this moment, Hawthorn eventually won this famous duel by just one second.

Far right: 1955, Monaco Grand Prix. The start of the race. (Left to right) Fangio (Mercedes), Ascari (Lancia), Moss (Mercedes). Fangio had to retire when in the lead.

which were to count for the newly instituted drivers' world championship. With three Grand Prix victories, Fangio came second. The following year, driving the fabulous Alfa Romeo 159, the title was his.

At the end of 1951, Alfa Romeo withdrew from Grand Prix racing. The next season was disastrous for Fangio. In June, when desperately overtired he crashed his Maserati at Monza and cracked several vertebrae in his neck. He was unable to race again that season. But he was back in 1953 and, although he won only one Grand Prix, he was second to Alberto Ascari in the world championship.

For the next four years, he dominated Grand Prix racing, winning the world championship with Maserati and Mercedes-Benz in 1954 and Mercedes-Benz in 1955, with Ferrari in 1956 and Maserati in 1957. During this period, he had many memorable victories.

In the 1953 Italian Grand Prix, for all 80 laps of the Monza circuit a fierce battle raged between Ascari and Giuseppe Farina in their Ferraris and Fangio and his fellow Argentinian, Onofre Marimón, in their Maseratis. As the four cars entered the final right-hander, Ascari was in the lead. Then his Ferrari was rammed by Marimón's Maserati. Both cars spun into the middle of the track. Farina was too close to avoid them and his Ferrari clipped one of the Maserati's wheels. Seizing his opportunity, Fangio slipped round the inside and came out of the corner comfortably in the

JUAN MANUEL FANGIO

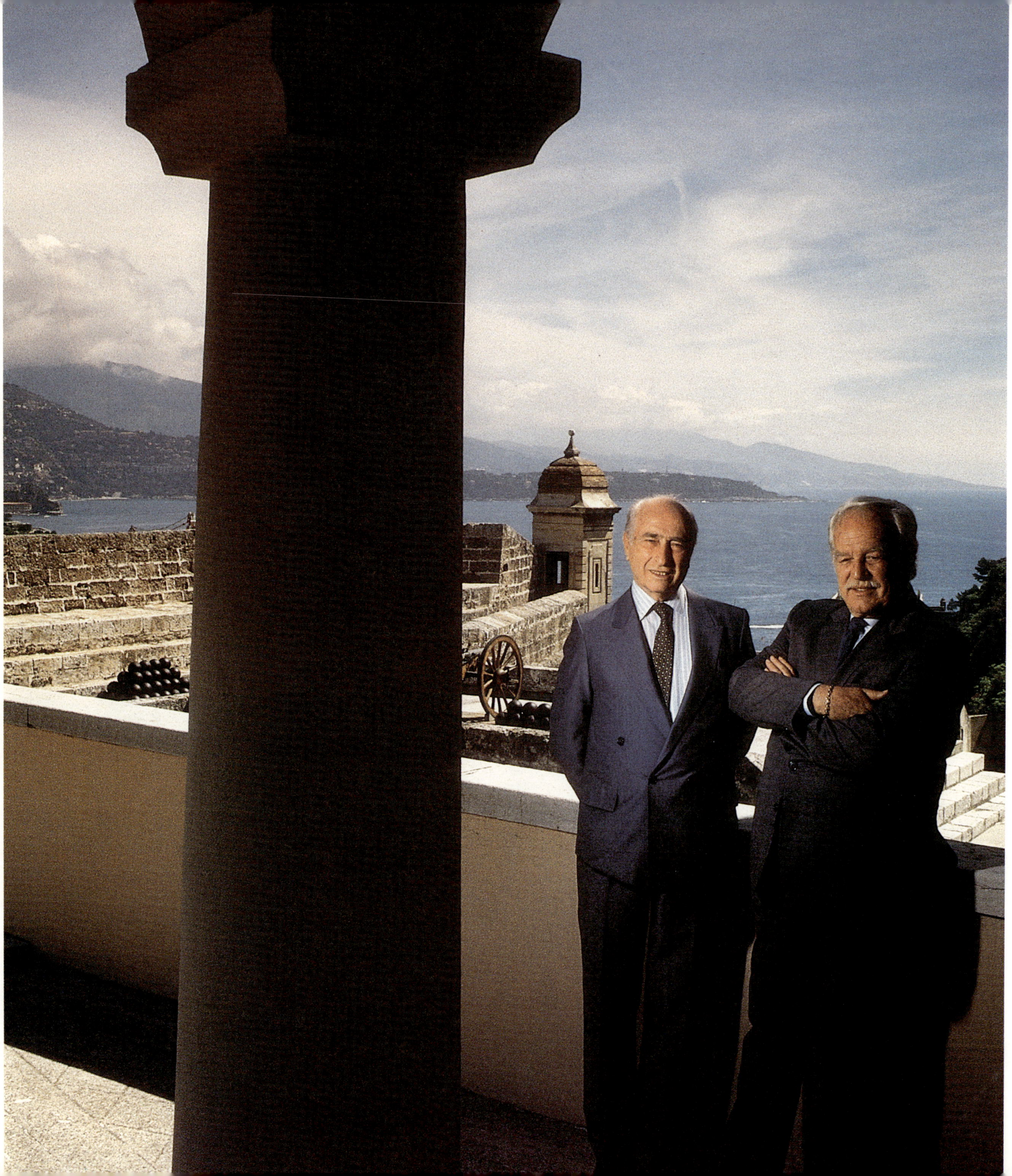

Over the years many motoring magazines have featured Fangio on their covers.

Left: Fangio with Prince Rainier at the Palace, Monaco, during his 1990 visit.

1957, German Grand Prix, Nürburgring. A crowded field at the start of the race, with protagonists Mike Hawthorn, Peter Collins and Fangio already getting to grips.

The chequered flag comes down on Fangio's last Grand Prix victory which also clinched his fifth world championship. Fangio recalled: 'I was quite inspired that day.'

John Surtees remembers that just after he had signed with Ferrari, Fangio uttered this warning: 'Be careful, John, it can be very dangerous there.' These words were to be especially significant for Surtees in 1966.

lead. The official was so surprised not to see a tight bunch of cars come out of the bend that he forgot to wave the chequered flag. So Fangio did another lap just to make sure of victory!

Possibly Fangio's greatest victory was the 1957 German Grand Prix. The Ferrari team decided to race non-stop, but Fangio chose to start with only half a tankful of fuel and to change tyres at half-distance. His pit-stop was inexplicably slow and he restarted 48 seconds behind the two Ferraris of Mike Hawthorn and Peter Collins. There were ten laps to go and, for the last nine of these, Fangio broke the lap record each time, snatching an incredible victory from the two Englishmen. 'I believe I was inspired that day,' Fangio has said.

'I never drove quite like that before and I never drove quite like it ever again.'

That race, in which he smashed the previous lap record by a staggering 11 seconds, secured Fangio's fifth world championship. It was also his last world championship victory. After a few races at the beginning of the 1958 season, he retired. He was 46 years old.

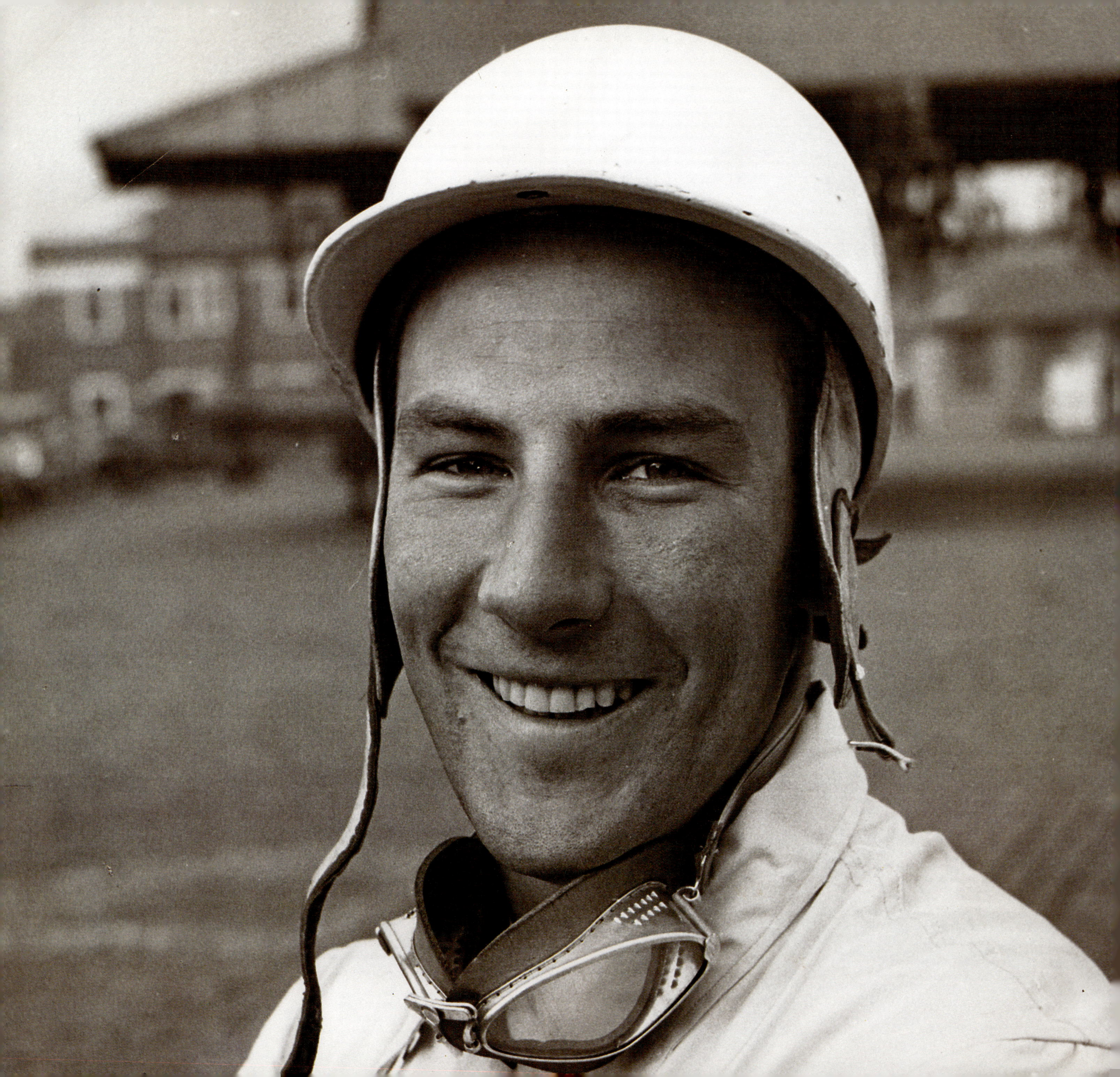

STIRLING MOSS

Often described as the greatest driver never to win the world championship, Stirling was a real competitor. Throughout his career he never stopped competing, and was perhaps at his best when he knew he had to make up for an inferior car. Stirling has always been universally admired, not least for the way he fought for his life after a near fatal crash in 1962 brought his racing career to a premature end.

As soon as I became involved in motor racing, I established many links with Stirling. In October 1959, before I'd seriously contemplated making the switch from two wheels to four, I was invited to test drive an Aston Martin—the DBR1 in which Stirling had won the Nürburgring 1000 km. It was against his lap times that mine were measured.

Still far from certain I would take up motor racing, I agreed, in January 1960, to do another test drive. This time it was for Tony Vandervell in one of the 1958 Vanwalls which Stirling and Tony Brooks had driven with such success.

I then decided to race cars whenever my motor-cycling commitments allowed, and over the next few months I had the opportunity to watch Stirling at work at Silverstone, Portugal, Monte Carlo and Aintree. Observing him at close quarters like this made me realise that he was the one to beat.

So I developed, and have maintained ever since the highest respect for Stirling. He was a great competitor and loved motor racing. For much of his time with Maserati and Mercedes he was, to some degree,

Above top: 1955, Mille Miglia. Stirling on his way to what was arguably his greatest victory.
Above: 1955 Targa Florio. Stirling drives the Mercedes 300SLR in which he secured a dramatic victory. His co-driver was Peter Collins.

overshadowed by Fangio. Stirling was runner-up to him in the world championships of 1955, 1956 and 1957. In 1958, after Fangio's retirement, Stirling was again runner-up in the championship—to Mike Hawthorn. In the following three seasons, he was third.

One of his most memorable racing achievements was the 1955 Mille Miglia when, with his navigator Denis Jenkinson who had been passenger to 1949 world sidecar champion Eric Oliver, he became the first and only Briton to win the classic Italian road race. Their preparation was meticulous. For weeks they'd driven the route, charting every hazard and corner. By the start, Jenkinson had a vast scroll of detailed information in a specially-designed aluminium holder. They'd also rehearsed fifteen different hand signals.

There were 533 cars in the race which left the start one-by-one in close succession. Stirling, in his 300 SLR Mercedes-Benz, was one of the last to go. After just over ten hours, Stirling was the victor, more than 30 minutes ahead of the second car, a similar Mercedes driven by Fangio.

Ten weeks later, Stirling again beat Fangio—this time in the British Grand Prix at Aintree. From the start, the race was a battle between the two silver Mercedes W196s of Fangio, the acknowledged master, and Moss, his team-mate, who was nearly 20 years younger.

Far right: 1955, Eifel sports car race, Nürburgring. Moss with his hero Fangio after their 1-2 victory.

Above top: 1952, Sports Car Grand Prix, Monaco. Stirling with his C-type Jaguar which was eliminated from the race in a multiple pile-up.
Above: 1957, Italian Grand Prix, Monza. Moss in his Vanwall during a pit-stop. Stirling's victory was the fulfilment of Tony Vandervell's dream of beating the Italians on their home ground.

57

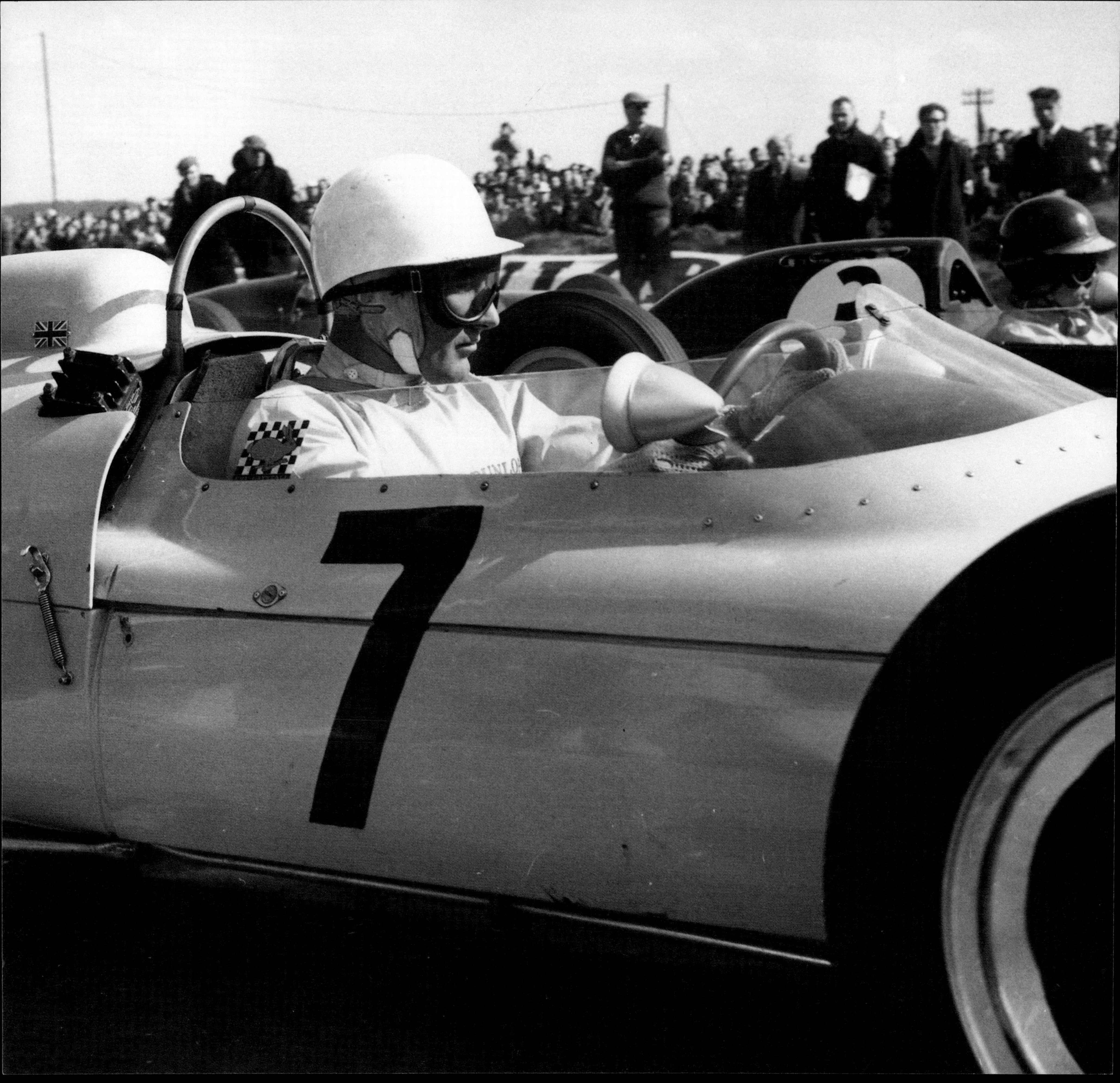
7

Left: April 1962, Lombank Trophy, Snetterton. Moss in the Lotus-Climax, only days before the horrendous Goodwood accident brought his illustrious career to an end.

1957, Pescara Grand Prix. Moss and Fangio in animated discussion after Stirling's win for Vanwall.

Right: 1957, British Grand Prix, Aintree. Stirling in the Vanwall on his way to an historic victory. Moss was the first Briton to win the British Grand Prix in a British car.

At the flag, Fangio sprinted into the lead. On the third lap, Stirling overtook him. On lap 17, Fangio surged to the front, but nine laps later Stirling recaptured the lead and appeared to be getting away. But Fangio closed little by little and, as they entered the final lap, the two Mercedes were nose-to-tail. As they took the chequered flag, Stirling was ahead, but by only half a car's length.

It may not have been in a British car, but Stirling's victory before his home crowd was greeted with delirious enthusiasm. As a tribute, he presented his winner's laurels to Fangio. Did the master, on this occasion, allow his pupil to win? Stirling has never been sure. Only Fangio knows for certain.

There are no doubts about Stirling's third win at Monte Carlo in 1961. It was one of his greatest drives. That year, the new 1.5-litre regulations had been introduced for Formula One. While other manufacturers wasted their efforts in protests, Ferrari spent their time developing a new V6 engine. Stirling was pitted against the new Ferraris in Rob Walker's under-powered but superior-handling four-cylinder Lotus-Climax. On lap 11, Moss wrested the lead from American Richie Ginther, the new boy in the Ferrari team.

For the remaining 89 laps, Stirling used all his precision and anticipation to weave in and out of backmarkers and keep his leading position. At the chequered flag, Ginther was only 3.6 seconds behind. 'If you do well against Stirling,' the American said, 'you know you've done something real special.'

STIRLING MOSS

23 April 1962, Glover Trophy, Goodwood. Stirling driving the Lotus-Climax shortly before the crash that ended his racing career. It is ironic that the car carried his lucky number 7.

9 June 1962. Stirling in the grounds of Atkinson Morley's Hospital, Wimbledon. His paralysed left side has responded to treatment, and the sense of fun and mental energy that are so characteristic of him show that he is well on his way to recovery after his Easter Monday crash.

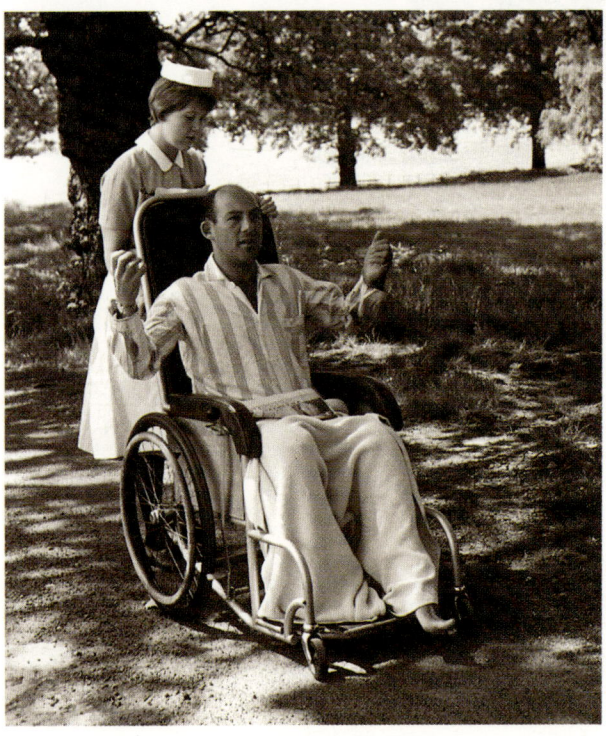

On Easter Monday 1962, Stirling and I were both driving in the Glover Trophy at Goodwood. We both had to pit with car problems, but once back on the track we were competing for the fastest lap, each taking it back from the other as the laps went by. Then Stirling, in his endeavour to pass the leader, Graham Hill, had his terrible crash. It took 40 minutes to cut him from the wreckage. For a week he was unconscious and, for much longer, his whole left side was paralysed, but, with the same determination he'd shown as a driver, he fought back to fitness.

A year later, after a test drive in a Lotus, he announced his retirement from racing.

17 April 1980. Stirling and Susie Moss on the balcony at Crockfords, at the evening party held to celebrate their wedding earlier the same day.

1989, Pirelli Classic Marathon. Stirling drove with American journalist Jean Lindamood.

JACK BRABHAM

Driving the revolutionary rear-engined Cooper-Climax, Jack Brabham won the Formula One World Championship in both 1959 and 1960. Six years later, at the age of 40, he made history by becoming the first driver to win the world title in a car of his own design and construction.

Jack Brabham in a Cooper-Climax early in his single-seater career.

In 1955, Jack arrived in England with his wife, Betty, and his eight-year-old son, Geoffrey. In Australia, he'd made a name for himself racing first American-style midget cars and then modified Coopers in hillclimbs. Despite these successes, he was unknown in Europe and soon found the standard of motor racing was much higher than it had been at home, but this made him even more determined to succeed.

He bought and quickly resold the ex-Peter Whitehead Cooper-Alta. Realizing he must have a viable racing car, he visited the Cooper Car Company in Surbiton where he met Charles Cooper and his son, John. It was the start of a long and successful association.

Jack persuaded the Coopers to let him build a Bristol-engined version of their 'bob-tailed' centre-seat sports car. Driving it at Snetterton, in his second race, he had a marvellous battle for third place with Stirling Moss in his 250F Maserati. It was enough to convince Jack he could succeed in Europe and so, at the end of the season, he returned temporarily to Australia with his wife and young son.

He took the Cooper-Bristol with him and in it won the Australian Grand Prix. Arriving back in England, early in 1956, he bought the ex-Rubery Owen 250F Maserati, but disposed of the car again after only a couple of races. John Cooper then offered him his first works drive in one of the Surbiton factory's single-seater sports cars.

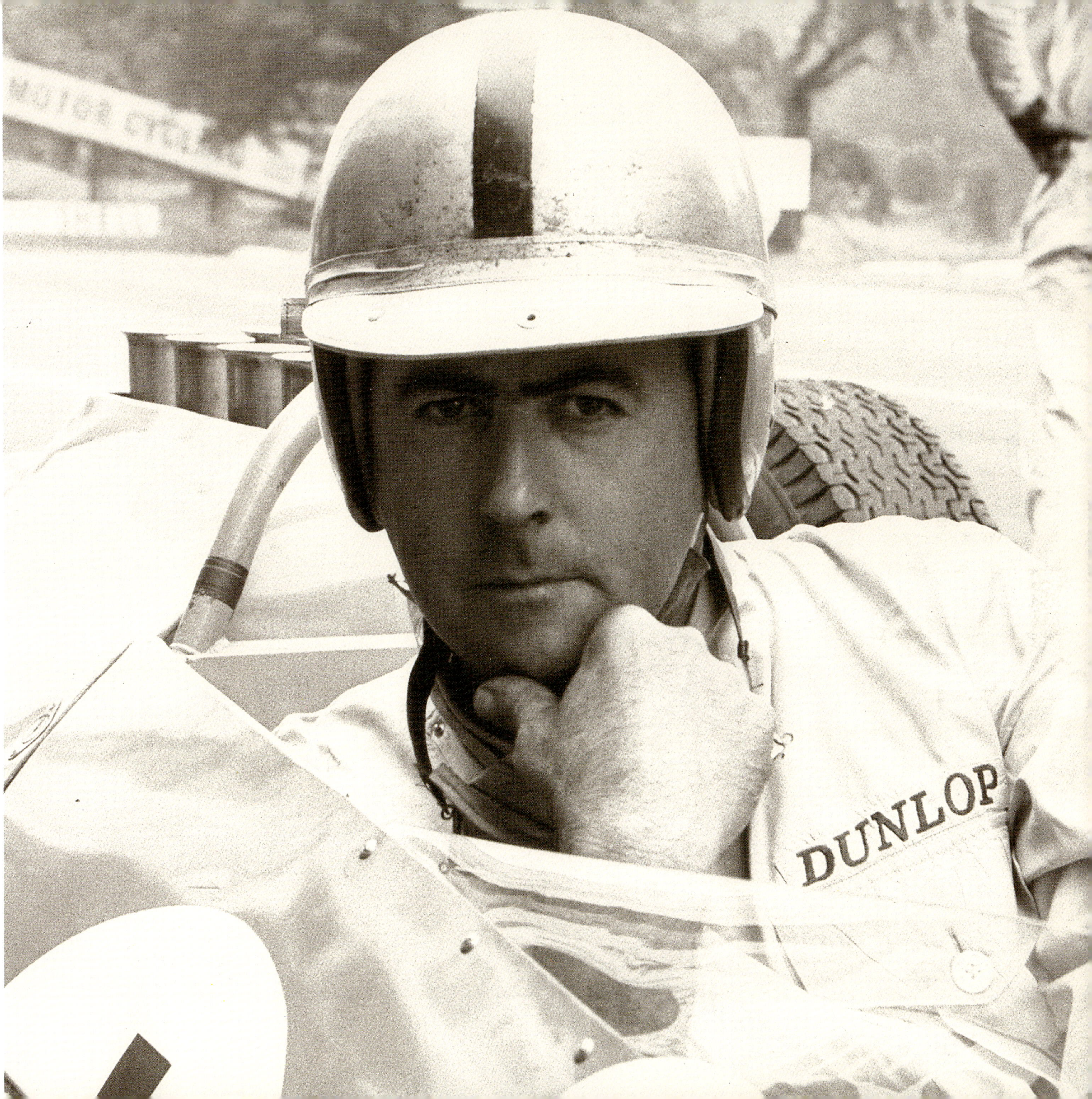

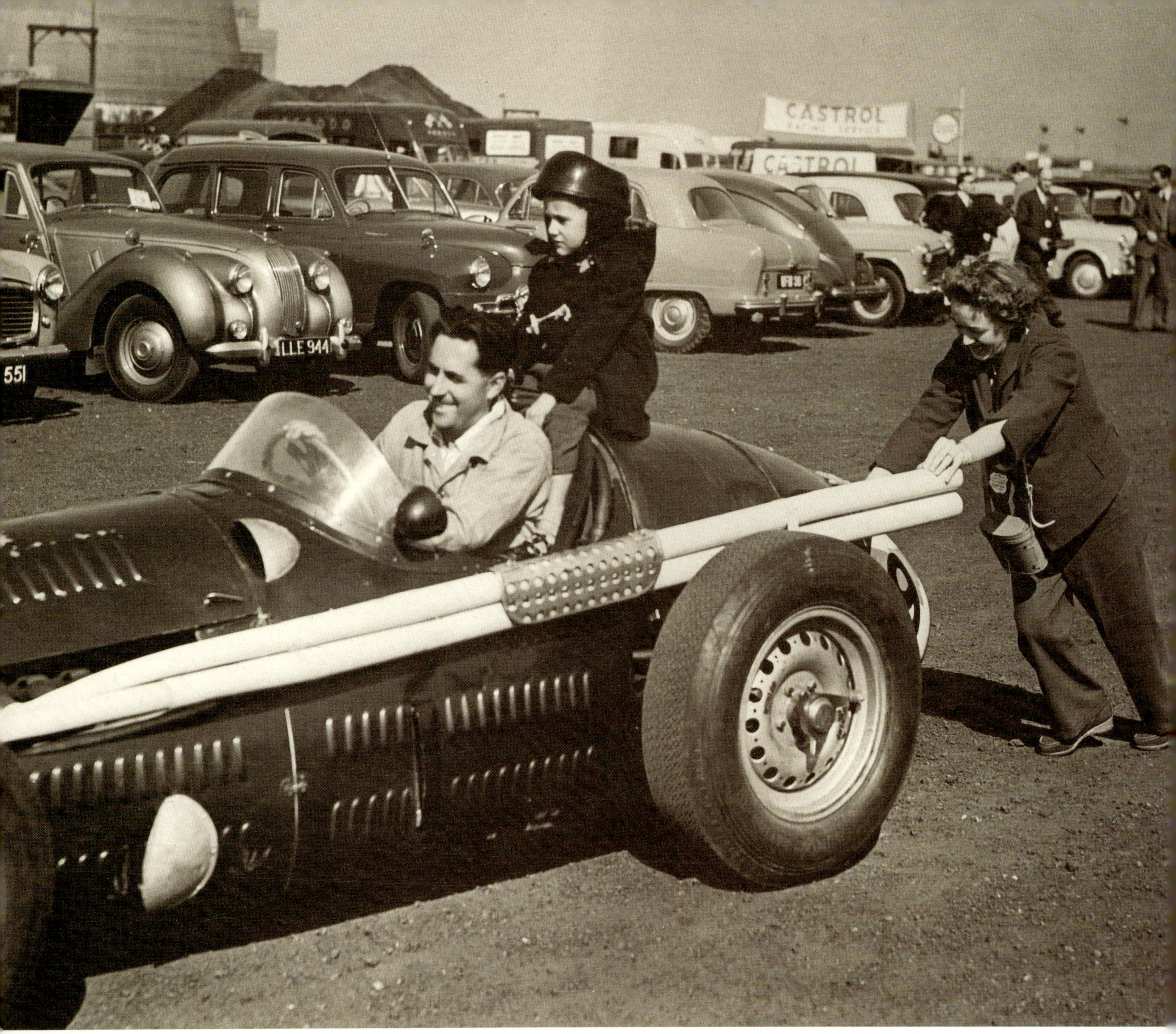
CASTROL
CASTROL
LLE 944
551

Left: Brabham and his son Geoffrey in a 250F Maserati get a push from Jack's wife Betty.

Right: 1964, US Grand Prix, Watkins Glen. (Left to right) Dan Gurney (Brabham), Trevor Taylor (Lotus), Jack Brabham (Brabham) and winner Graham Hill (BRM). Gurney, who had joined Brabham the previous year, scored two victories for Jack during the season, in France and in Mexico.

In 1957, Jack had a full Formula One season, driving a 2.2-litre Cooper-Climax. He had no Grand Prix victories, but he captured public attention at Monte Carlo. In practice, he crashed into the barriers at the Casino—'Just trying to get in for nothing,' he said cheerily. Then, in the race itself, he was lying third shortly before the finish when the fuel pump mounting broke. Jack leapt out and pushed the Cooper home to finish sixth. He was fourth at Monte Carlo the following year and gained his first world championship points, but they were to be all he scored that season.

Things were very different in 1959. Back at Monte Carlo, Jack won his first Grand Prix. He came second at Zandvoort and had a start-to-finish win in the British Grand Prix at Aintree. In the final race of the season, the United States Grand Prix at Sebring, his Cooper-Climax was in the lead on the final lap when it ran out of fuel. Bruce McLaren, Jack's team-mate, was the surprised winner, while Jack pushed his car across the line to finish fourth. The three points he won were sufficient to make him the 1959 world champion.

It was during the 1960 season that I first met Jack, for I had begun to race in the occasional Formula One event when my motorcycle contracts allowed. Driving a works Lotus, I actually finished second behind him in my second Grand Prix—the British, at Silverstone.

It was one of Jack's five straight victories which ensured he won his second, consecutive title.

In 1961, the much criticized 1.5-litre formula was introduced and Cooper, like most British teams, was woefully ill-prepared. Jack finished the season with only four championship points. He did, however, cause

Far right: 15 November 1966, Buckingham Palace, London. Jack with his wife Betty and son Geoffrey. This was the year of Jack's four successive Grand Prix wins in the new Brabham-Repco, and his third world championship. Brabham was the first ever to win the championship in a car bearing his own name.

Brands Hatch. Jack Brabham in the Brabham.

a sensation in the Indianapolis 500 when he came ninth in the little 2.7-litre mid-engined Cooper-Climax which heralded the demise of the traditional front-engined Indy roadster.

At the end of the 1961 season, Jack left Cooper to start building his own racing cars. With his fellow Australian, Ron Tauranac, as his chief designer, Jack manufactured a conventional multi-tubular chassis, powered by the 1.5-litre Coventry-Climax V8. For the first half of 1962 he raced a privately-entered Lotus, and the new Brabham made its debut at the German Grand Prix, but had to retire with a broken throttle linkage.

It was to be another two years before Dan Gurney scored the first Grand Prix victory for Brabham.

The unpopular 1.5-litre formula was abandoned for 1966 and the maximum engine capacity was raised to 3 litres. As Coventry-Climax announced it was pulling out of racing, Jack had to search for an alternative engine. He opted for a 3-litre V8, originally built by General Motors, which was modified for racing by the brilliant Phil Irving of the Australian firm, Repco. Irving had made his name as designer of the Vincent, HRD and Velocette motorcycles.

Jack drove the new Brabham-Repco to four

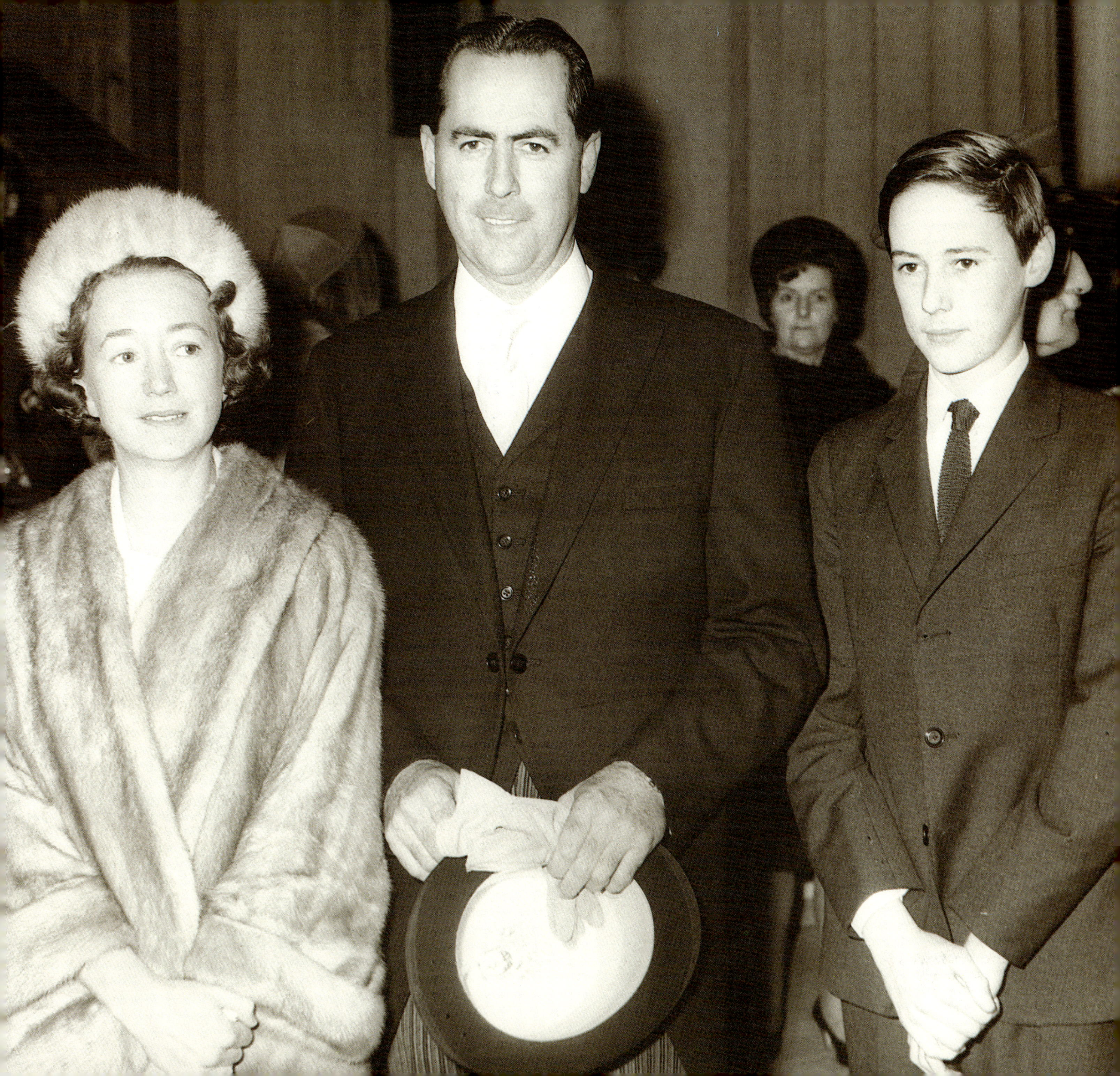

Jack's mechanical expertise played a large part in his success.

John Surtees remembers that the renaissance of British motor racing which had begun in the mid-1950s was by no means due to the large, long-established companies. It had grown out of the small workshops of giants such as John Cooper, Colin Chapman (Lotus) and Tony Vandervell (Vanwall). Further backing came from Leonard Lord and Wally Hassan (Coventry-Climax) and, later, Keith Duckworth (Cosworth). Jack Brabham was another of these inspirational pioneers, displaying typically Australian spirit and tenacity.

JACK BRABHAM

successive Grand Prix wins and his third world championship, becoming the first driver ever to secure the title in a car bearing his own name. The following year, he was runner-up in the world championship to his new teammate, Denny Hulme, and the Brabham team won the Constructors' Cup for the second year in succession.

At the end of the 1970 season, when he won in South Africa, Jack announced his retirement. He was 44 years old, had made 123 Grand Prix starts and won 14. It was the end of a significant era in motor racing.

Sir Jack Brabham, as he became, made a contribution to the sport that many people haven't fully appreciated. As an engineer, he was closely involved with the development of the revolutionary Cooper-Climax. As a businessman, he successfully manufactured his own racing cars and established a team which, under different ownership, was to win further world championships in 1981 and 1983 with Nelson Piquet.

Having lost the championship to Jack by 14 points in the 1966 season, despite my win in Belgium, I can say that he was a tough competitor. He had a disarming twinkle in his eye, but that didn't fool many of us. You always had a fight on your hands when he was around. If you were using all the road to try and stop him coming through, you had to use some of the off-road area too, because otherwise he certainly would.

69

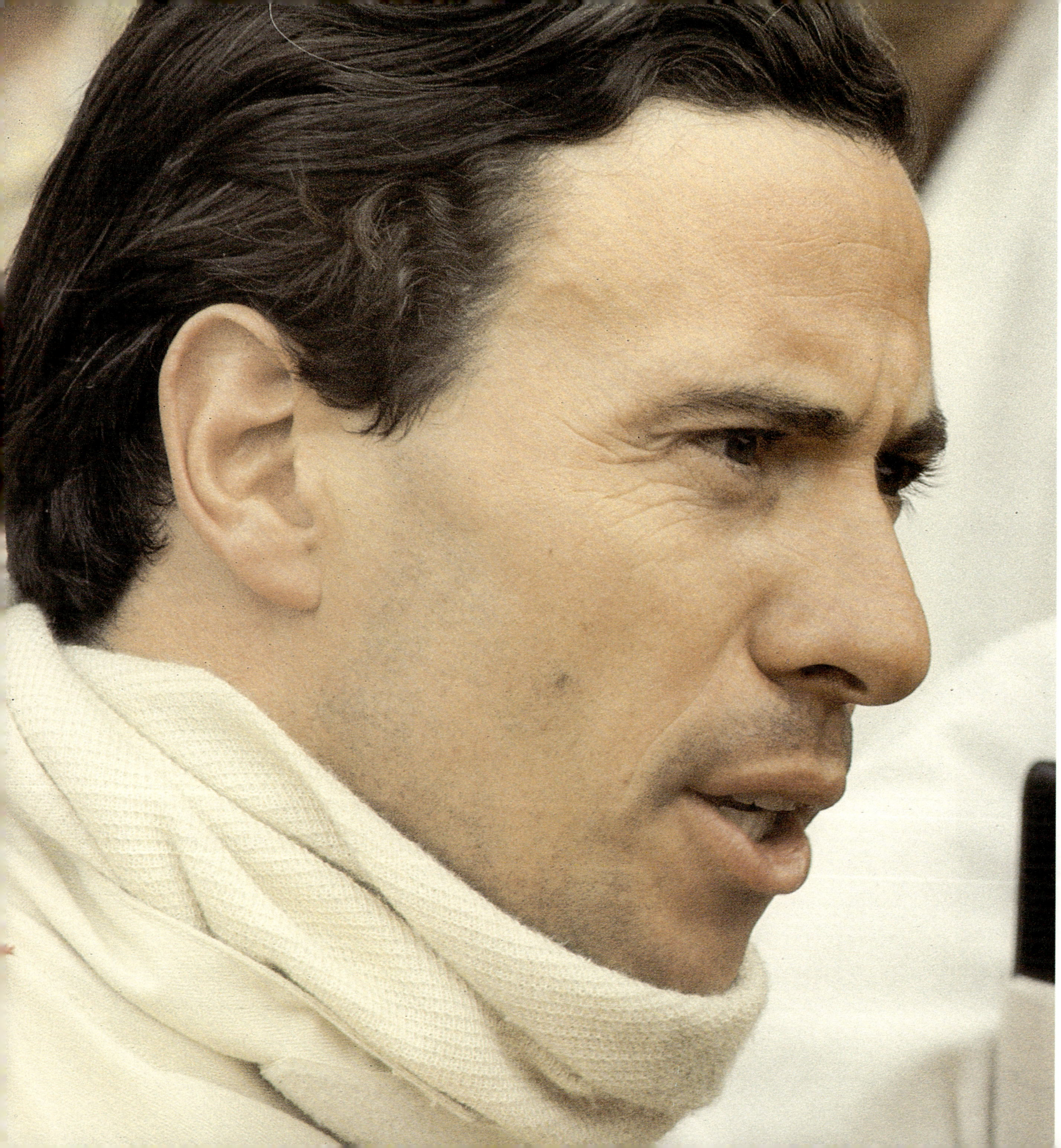

JIM CLARK

Reserved and unassuming off the track, Jim Clark was unquestionably one of the greatest drivers of all time. His partnership with Colin Chapman, the engineering genius behind Lotus cars, was one of the closest and most consistently successful in Formula One history. Twice world champion, Clark tragically died after a racing accident in 1968.

In a way, my motor racing life started with Jim Clark. I'd never seen a car race before I competed in one—a Formula Junior event at Goodwood on 19 March 1960. I was driving for Ken Tyrrell and my main competitor was Jim in the works Lotus. After a great battle with him, I came second.

Colin Chapman then asked me to join his Formula One Lotus team with Innes Ireland. As I was still committed to my motorcycling career, it was agreed that, when I wasn't available, either Alan Stacey or Jim would drive in my place.

My first Formula One Grand Prix was at Monte Carlo in May 1960, where I failed to finish. I wasn't available for either the Dutch or the Belgian Grand Prix, both of which took place in June, so Jim had his first Formula One outing in Holland.

For the next race at the Spa circuit, three Lotus cars were entered, driven by Ireland, Stacey and Jim. Sadly, Stacey lost control and was killed. Jim finished fifth, collecting his first world championship points, but the death of his team-mate shattered any enjoyment he might otherwise have felt.

Above top: September 1960, Snetterton, the paddock. Clark in an F1 Lotus.
Above: 1962, British Grand Prix, Aintree. The Lotus 25.

13 September 1963. Jimmy Clark, sheep farmer, at the sheep sales, Kelso, Scotland. Later that day Clark exchanged cloth cap for helmet and returned to Brands Hatch for a demonstration drive.

October 1963, US Grand Prix, Watkins Glen. Clark in the Lotus 25.

At the end of the season, Jim, Innes Ireland and I flew to America to take part in the Grand Prix at Riverside, a desert circuit. I made a bad start, but had begun to make up ground when I made the mistake of leaving the clean track while overtaking Jim. I lost control on the dirt, and took us both out of the race. I wasn't very popular for a while, mainly with Ireland, because he, Jim and I had agreed to pool the large prize money for this race and my error meant that he was the only one of us left. He finished second and had to share his winnings with Jim and me. He was not pleased!

At the end of the season, Chapman offered me the number one seat at Lotus for 1961 and my own choice of team-mate. I chose Jim. Over the next few weeks a row instigated by Innes developed between him, Chapman and myself, as a result of which I decided to walk away. I joined the Yeoman Credit team of Coopers run by Reg Parnell. Jim sensibly stayed with Chapman, despite approaches from other teams, including Ferrari and Porsche. Although no longer team-mates, he and I remained friends and, when I first married in 1962, Jim was my best man.

In 1961, new Formula One regulations came into force, reducing the maximum capacity of Grand Prix cars from 2.5 to 1.5 litres. Unlike the other manufacturers, apart from Ferrari, Chapman had his new car ready—the Lotus 21. Jim and Ireland battled hard throughout the season, but it was the crimson Ferraris

Right: 1963, Italian Grand Prix, Monza. Jim Clark takes Lotus boss Colin Chapman on a lap of honour after his win in the Lotus 25.

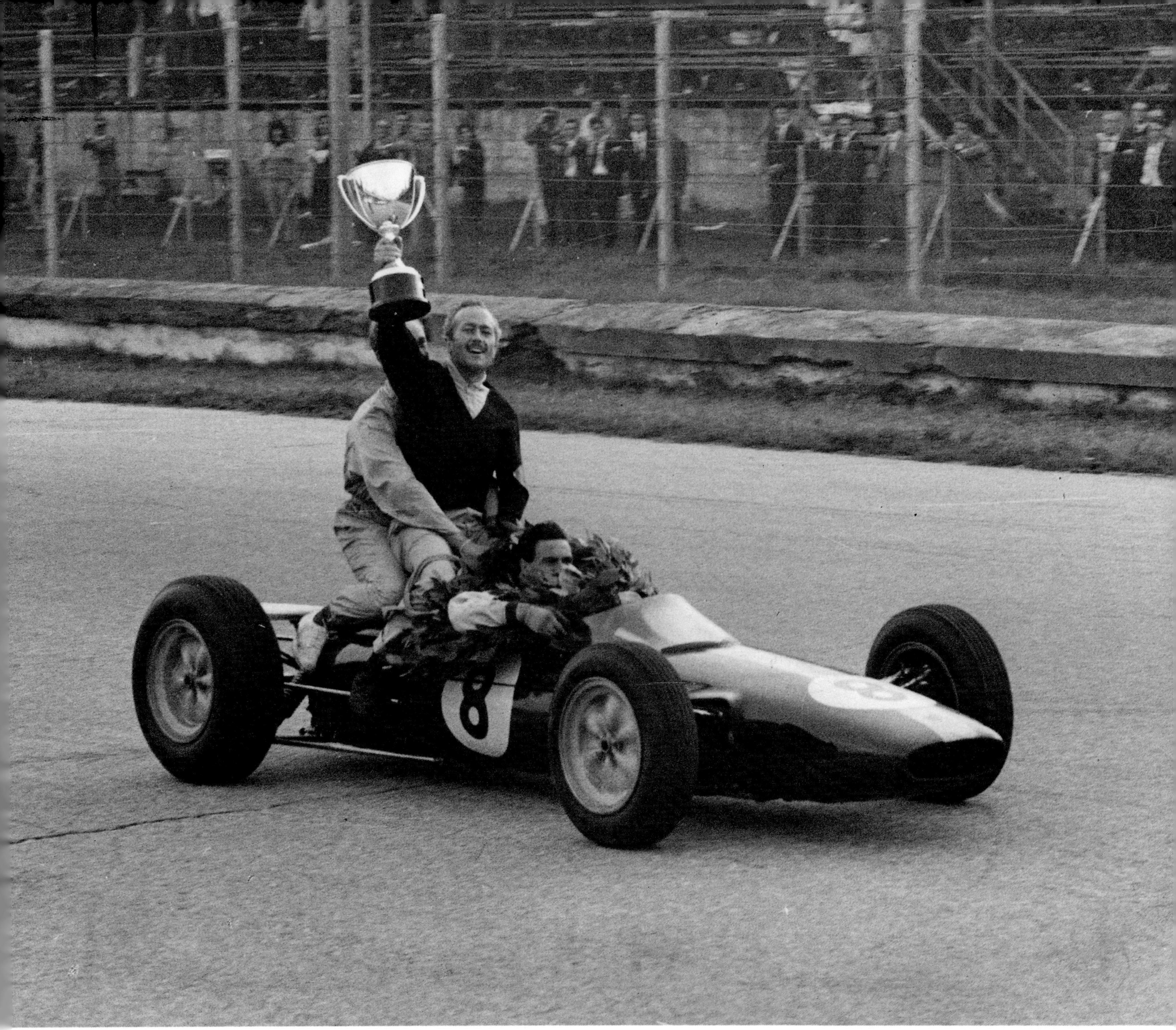

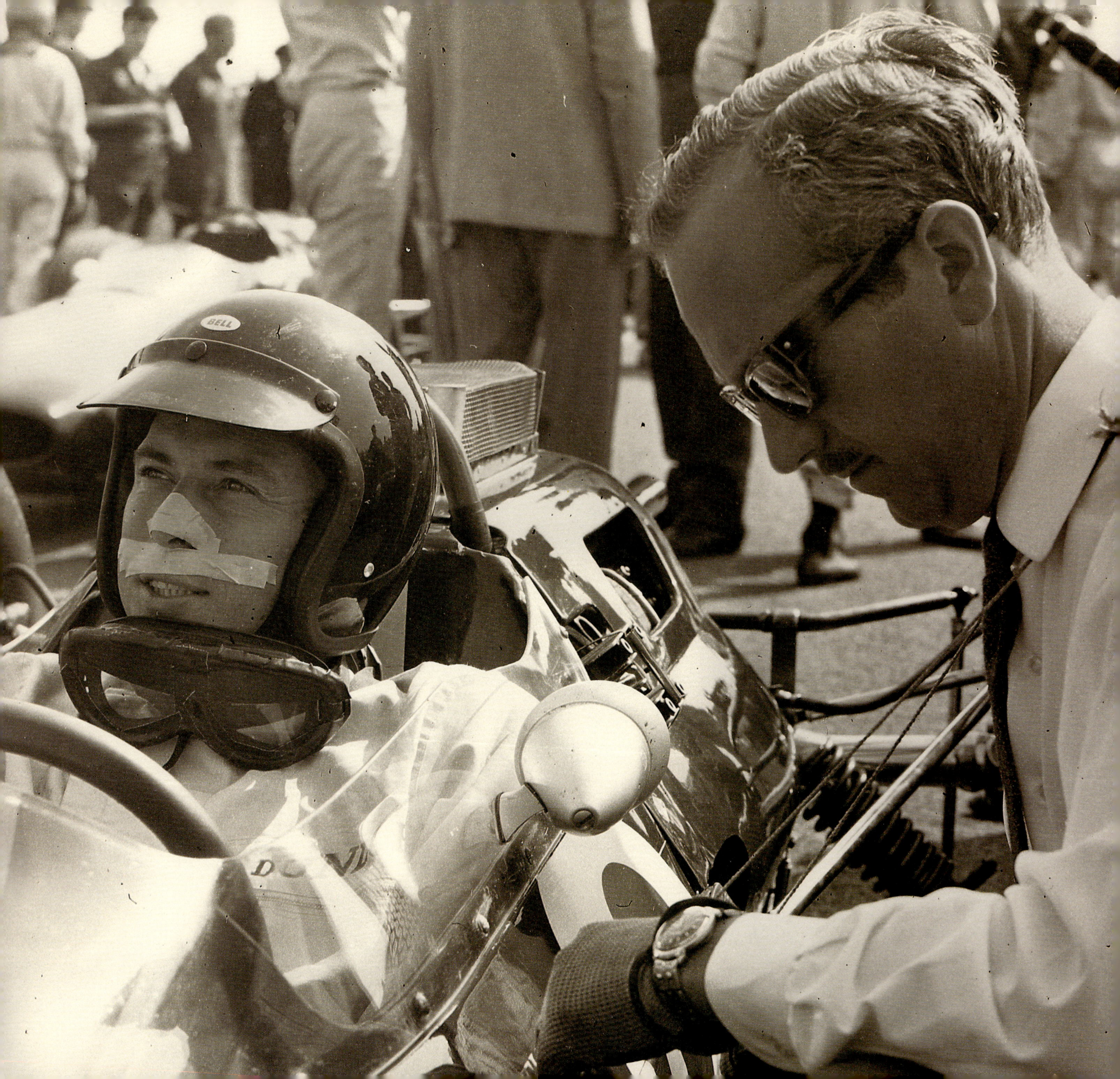
BELL

Left: The partnership between Colin Chapman (right) and Jim Clark proved to be one of the most formidable in Grand Prix racing.

Jim Clark and the Lotus 25—an almost unbeatable combination.

1967, Tasman Series. Jim celebrates another victory.

that romped home with the championship honours.

Before the next season opened, Chapman made the decision he had wanted to make during 1961—he did not renew Ireland's contract. It was Jim who successfully led the Lotus team for 1962, winning three Grands Prix and finishing runner-up in the world championship to Graham Hill in the BRM V8. Throughout that year Jim was driving the Lotus 25 with its innovative monocoque design. As he was to do throughout Jim's racing career, Chapman had designed the car around the Scot's 5ft 7in (1.70m) frame.

The degree of confidence built up between the two men forged a close and highly successful relationship that was unique in motor sport history. Chapman was the most brilliant Grand Prix innovator of his time and Jim a very special driver. He was thoughtful and tough. I never found him the most forceful of drivers but, when he knew that his car was right, he was as hard to beat as a man could be.

Perhaps it was the support that this unusual relationship afforded him that enabled Clark to switch off after a race while most other drivers would anxiously run an action replay in their minds. Once the race was over, Jim would disappear back to his sheep farm and his beloved home town of Duns in the Scottish borders. I wondered at the way he managed to live two separate

JIM CLARK

lives. One moment he was Jim Clark, the glamorous Grand Prix driver, and the next he was Jimmy Clark, the bachelor sheep farmer.

For the next few years, the Lotus combination was the one to beat in motor racing. In 1963, Jim became the youngest-ever world champion with a record seven wins. In 1964, when I won the world championship, he was third. The following year, he not only won the title again with another six Grand Prix victories, he also became the first British driver to win the Indianapolis 500. In 1967, he won four Grands Prix.

His impressive run of successes continued. His win in the South African Grand Prix, the first of the 1968 season, took his tally of victories to 25—one more than the record number previously set by Fangio.

On 7 April 1968, during the sixth lap of a relatively unimportant Formula Two race at the Hockenheim circuit in Germany, Jim's Lotus-Cosworth inexplicably went out of control while coming out of a gentle right-hand curve at high speed. The car shot across the track and hurtled broadside into a clump of trees, disintegrating into a shower of wreckage. Jim died instantly. When I recall Clark's fatal accident, I am always reminded of an earlier crash, from which Jim escaped unscathed, because of what he said afterwards. He was talking to Basil Cardew, the motoring journalist, who must have been commiserating with him. 'Don't say it was back luck,' Jim responded. 'I don't believe in it. I must have done something wrong. I'll see it doesn't happen again.'

His death stunned the whole motor racing world. For many people, he represented the ideal sportsman—a talented driver who was polite, modest and so calm off the track that I've more than once had the impression that he'd wandered by accident into the hectic Grand Prix circus. It seemed impossible that such a tragic accident could have happened to such a man as Jim Clark.

1968, South African Grand Prix, Kyalami. This was to be Clark's last win.

Jim with Sally Stokes, his long-time girlfriend.

Far right: 1967, US Grand Prix, Watkins Glen. Winner Jim Clark with runner-up Graham Hill.

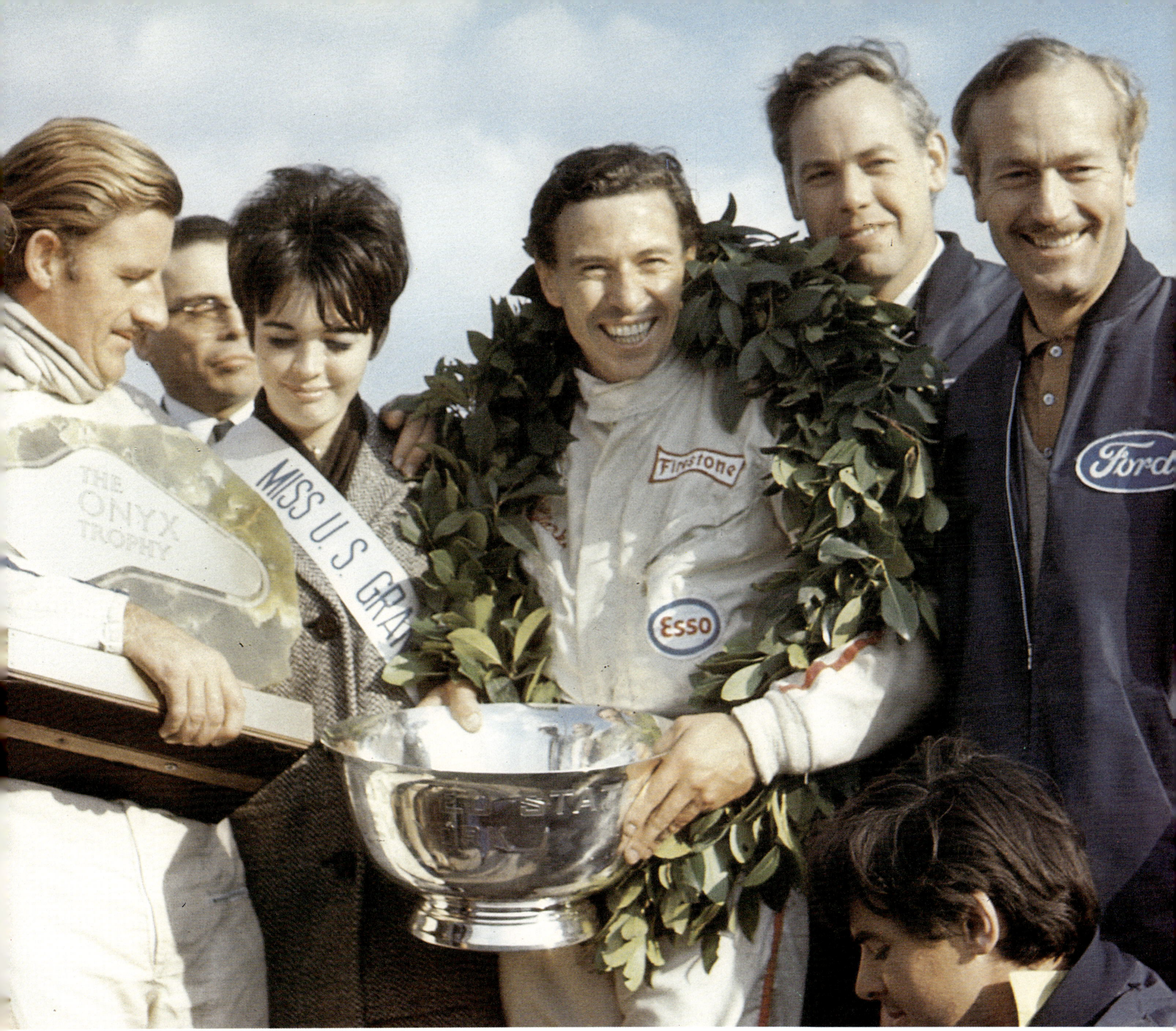
THE ONYX TROPHY
MISS U.S. GRAN
Firestone
Esso
Ford

GRAHAM HILL

Graham Hill was a universally popular racing driver. Determination and hard work, rather than just natural ability or luck, were responsible for his considerable achievements, which included two world championships. Good-humoured, articulate and approachable, he greatly enhanced the popularity and prestige of motor racing.

Graham Hill decided, at an early age, that he wanted to be an engineer. As a child, he loved tinkering with machinery bought from local secondhand shops. His National Service was spent as an engine-room artificer in the Royal Navy. Afterwards, he became an engineering apprentice with an instrument and accessories firm.

He began to take part in motorcycle scrambles and races. This came to an end when he was involved in a road accident which resulted in his being left with recurrent backache and a twisted left leg which settled an inch shorter than the right.

Not at all deterred by these injuries, Graham took up rowing. 'I was looking,' he later remarked jokingly, 'for a sport that I could do sitting down.' In 1952, he competed in the London Rowing Club's second eleven at Henley and, in 1953, he stroked their first eight to victory in the Grand Challenge Cup.

That same year, Graham, who was then 24, bought his first car (a 1934 Morris 8), taught himself to drive and scraped through his driving test. Shortly afterwards, during the winter break in the rowing season, he saw a driving school's advertisement offering

1962, German Grand Prix, Nürburgring. Graham Hill after one of his greatest victories.
Right: May 1959, Crystal Palace. Hill with a Lotus 15.

four laps around Brands Hatch. He went along and afterwards recalled, 'Until then I'd never seen a racing car but, after those four laps, I knew it was what I wanted to do with my life.'

He went back to Brands Hatch as often as he could, working as an unpaid mechanic in exchange for

78

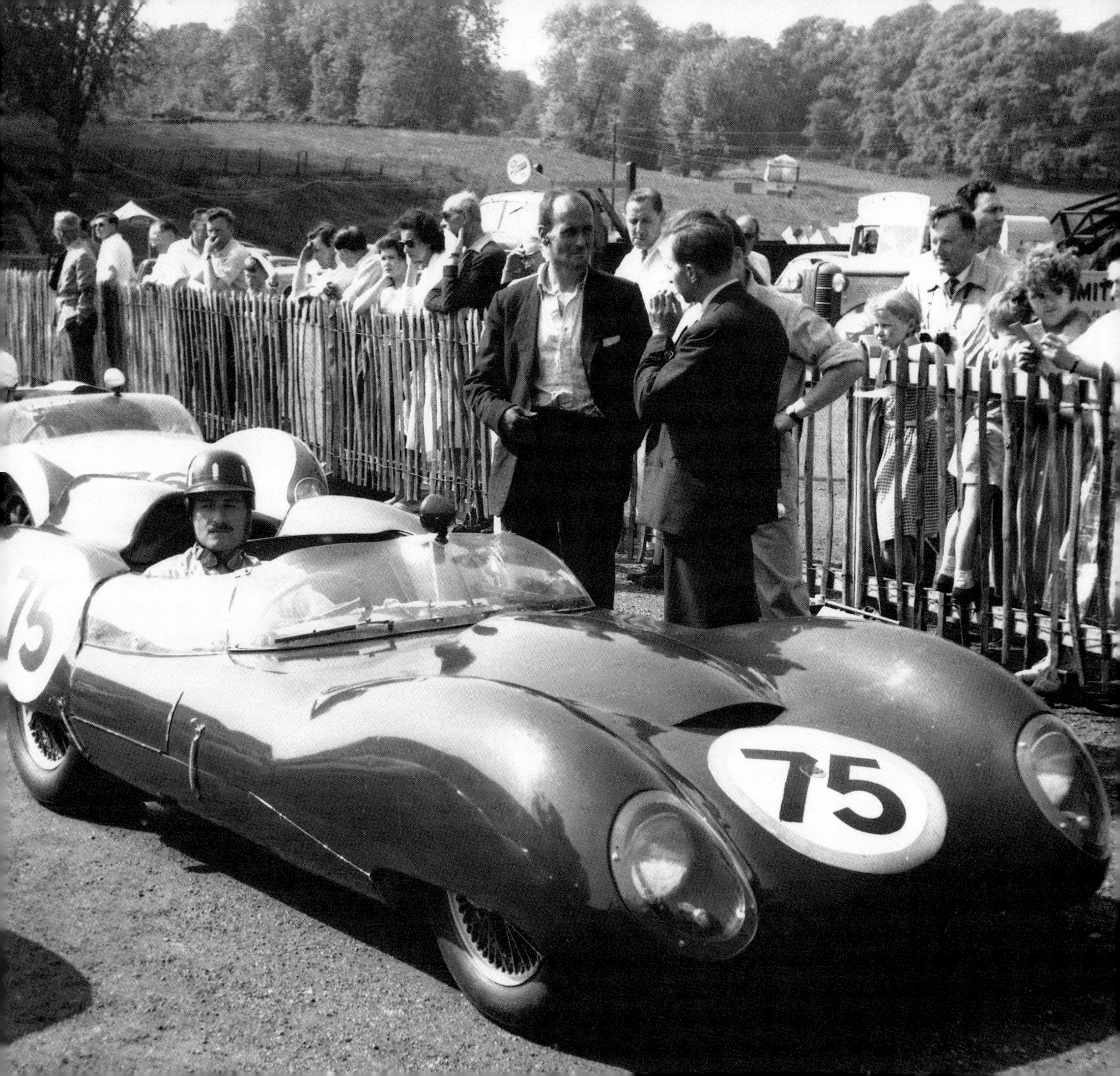
75

GRAHAM HILL

GRAHAM HILL

1965, British Grand Prix, Silverstone. Graham Hill before the race.

Left: 1966, Indianapolis 500. Hill in the Mecom Lola-Ford. Graham was one of the few drivers to win this race at his first attempt.

26 April 1966, Kodak House, London. Graham Hill opened an exhibition of motor racing photographs, and is seen here with a picture of Nuvolari taken in 1937.

drives. When the driving school unexpectedly went bankrupt, Graham gave up his engineering career and lived on unemployment benefit so that he could spend all his time trying to find a way into motor racing.

Hearing that a new driving school wanted a mechanic, he applied and got the job. At Brands Hatch in April 1954, he had his first race, driving a Cooper 500. He came second in the heat and fourth in the final. At an August race-meeting, he clambered into the transporter of the recently-formed Lotus team alongside Colin Chapman and Mike Costin. Neither of them asked who he was, because each assumed he was with the other. By the end of the journey, Graham had talked himself into a job as a mechanic with the team.

After three years preparing cars for private owners and enjoying the occasional drive, Graham left Lotus to join Speedwell Conversions, the North London tuning company. A year later, Chapman invited his ex-mechanic back to drive the new works Lotus in the 1958 Monaco Grand Prix. There was to be no fairy-tale beginning, for during the race, a halfshaft broke and the car shed a wheel.

However, at the age of 29, Graham had started his long and illustrious Grand Prix career, throughout which he wore what was to become his trademark—the famous dark blue racing helmet with its eight vertical white flashes, representing the blades of the London Rowing Club's first eight.

After two disappointing years, during which he didn't win a single championship point, Graham left Lotus to join BRM. Again, for a couple of years, results were slow in coming, but everything came right in 1962. Graham won four Grands Prix and the world championship. In 1963, 1964 and 1965, he was runner-up. In 1966, driving a Lola (which I should have driven but couldn't because of my accident in Canada), he became the first rookie since 1927 to win the Indianapolis 500.

GRAHAM HILL

In 1967, Graham returned to Team Lotus, where he joined Jim Clark. After Clark's death early in 1968 had shattered the team's morale, it was Graham who picked up the pieces and won his second world championship. In 1969, at Monte Carlo, he twice recorded the fastest time in practice and won his record fifth Monaco GP.

Later that year, in the United States Grand Prix at Watkins Glen, he crashed at 150 mph (241 kph) and broke both legs. Even though doctors pronounced that he wouldn't be fit again for at least a year, he promised he'd be back for the first race of the next season. Amazingly he was to keep his promise.

At the age of 41 and still in considerable pain, he had to be lifted into Rob Walker's privately-entered Lotus-Ford at the start of the South African Grand Prix. During the race, Graham paced himself expertly and, at the end, the crowd rose to cheer him as he

Brands Hatch. Graham relaxes between races with his daughters Brigitte and Samantha.

On the dodgems! Graham Hill, with Mrs John Campbell-Jones, does battle with Jim Clark and Mrs Gregor Grant.

1968. Graham Hill.

Hill after one of his five victories at Monaco.

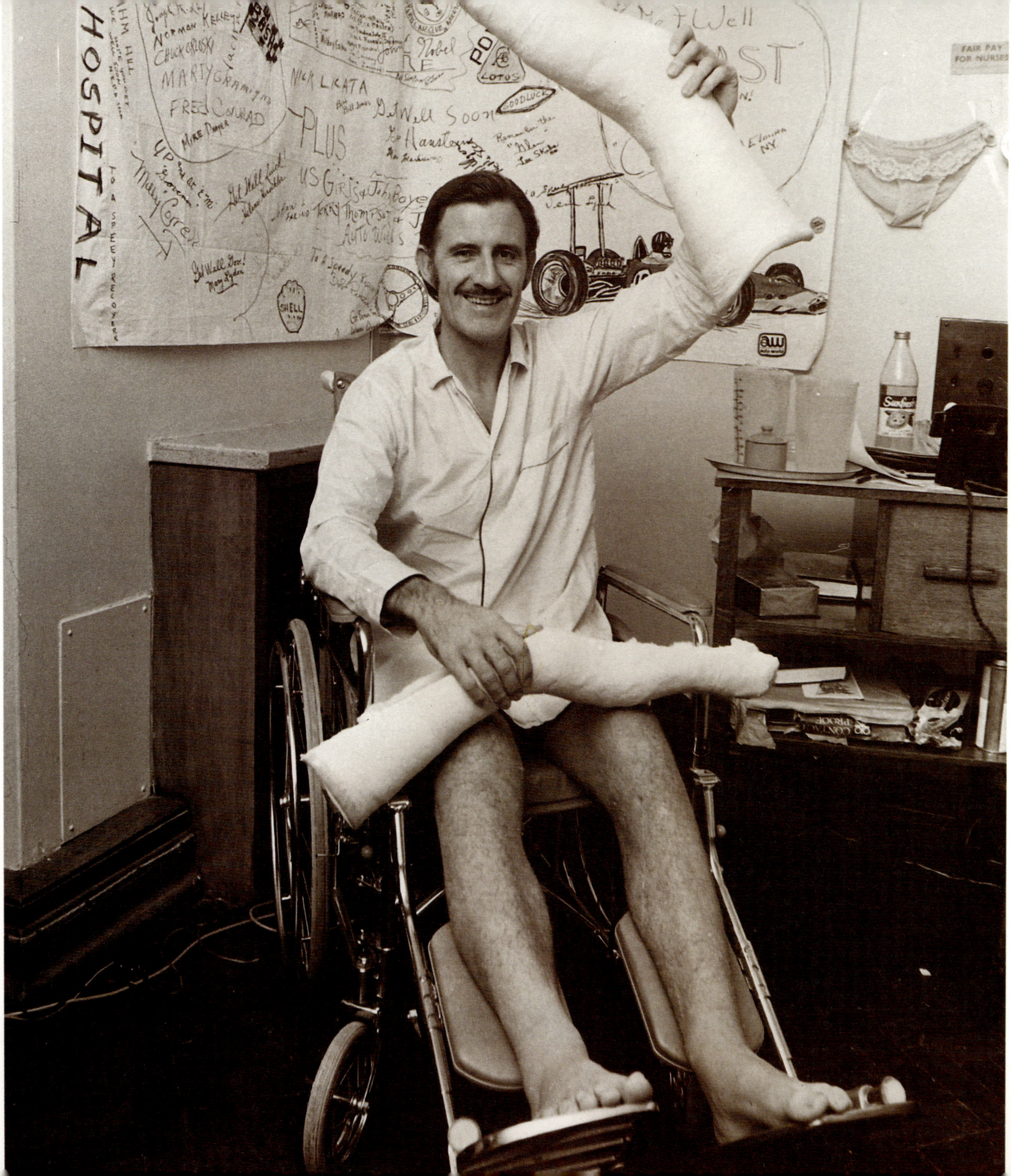
HOSPITAL
NORMAN KELLEY
CHUCK ORLOSKI
FRED CONRAD
PLUS
Get Well Soon
GOODLUCK
LOTUS
SHELL
FAIR PAY FOR NURSES

Left: Off comes the plaster some months after Graham's crash in October 1969 at the US Grand Prix, Watkins Glen.

Graham Hill with his friend actor Paul Newman, an accomplished racing driver Note the famous dark blue racing helmet with its eight vertical white flashes, representing the blades of the London Rowing Club's first eight.

finished exhausted but with a point for his sixth place.

Many of his friends and fans thought he should have retired that day, but Graham Hill loved motor racing too much to quit. Although he was not as fast as he had been and the drives came less frequently, he continued racing and, in 1972, won at Le Mans in a Matra-Simca, so becoming the first driver to achieve the triple distinction of winning the Formula One world championship, the Indianapolis 500 and Le Mans.

It was only in 1975 that he finally retired to concentrate on building up his own Grand Prix team. A few months later, the light plane he was piloting crashed. He and five key members of his team were killed.

Graham Hill was a gritty and determined driver and a much admired public figure. He was an eloquent and amusing public speaker and a practised campaigner for many causes and charities. With his death, motor racing lost a driver–statesman.

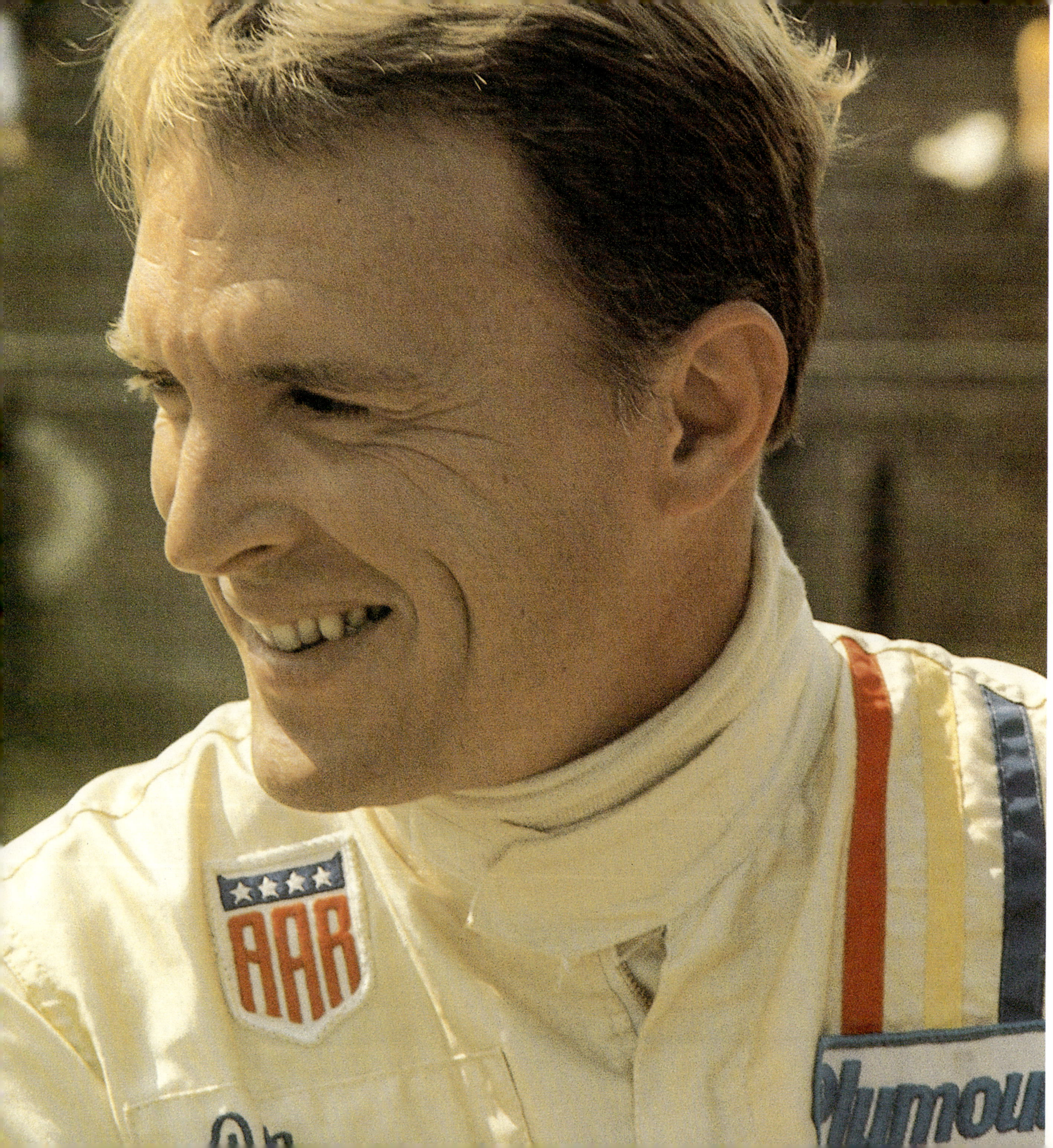
AAR

DAN GURNEY

Dan Gurney was the archetypal all-American hero. With his good looks, even temperament and huge driving talent, he was highly regarded by his fellow-drivers despite his frustrating race failures. In the event, he won many famous racing victories both in Europe and in America.

Son of an artistic mother and a father who was an opera singer, Dan Gurney might well never have taken up racing if he'd stayed in Long Island, New York, where he was born. But at the age of 17 he moved with his family to Riverside in California.

Motor racing was a growing craze on the West Coast and Dan was soon fascinated by it, although it was to be seven years before he drove in his first competition. During the following four years, he took part in 22 minor races, driving first his own Triumph TR2, then a Porsche, and finally Frank Arciero's 4.9-litre Ferrari. Several wins with this car in 1957 brought him to the attention of Luigi Chinetti who was prompted to sing his praises to Enzo Ferrari. His words must have been persuasive for Dan joined the Scuderia in 1959.

His first Grand Prix was at Reims in July. He was unplaced, but in his second race, the German Grand Prix, he finished second in a thrilling Ferrari 1-2-3.

1962, French Grand Prix, Rouen. Dan Gurney on his way to Porsche's one and only championship Grand Prix victory.

1962, US Grand Prix, Watkins Glen. Dan with Jim Clark and Graham Hill before the race.

1963, Indianapolis 500. Dan was instrumental in bringing Lotus and Ford together for their attack on this race, and is seen here in a Ford-engined Lotus 29

Far right: 1964, Mexican Grand Prix. Dan Gurney (left) being congratulated on his win by the Duke of Edinburgh. John Surtees (right) clinched the world championship at this event.

Later, he was third in Portugal and fourth at Monza.

For many drivers, to join the Ferrari team would be the climax of a career. For Dan, it was but the beginning. At the end of the season, he decided to move to BRM for 1960, but it was to be an unhappy association. He finished only once and crashed during the Dutch Grand Prix. He escaped with a broken arm, but sadly a spectator was killed as a result of the incident.

For 1961, Gurney joined Porsche. In the two seasons he was with them, he had some success, including a win in the 1962 French Grand Prix at Rouen, but this period brought significant reminders of what might have been. In 1961, Phil Hill won the world championship and Ferrari won the Constructors' Cup. The

89

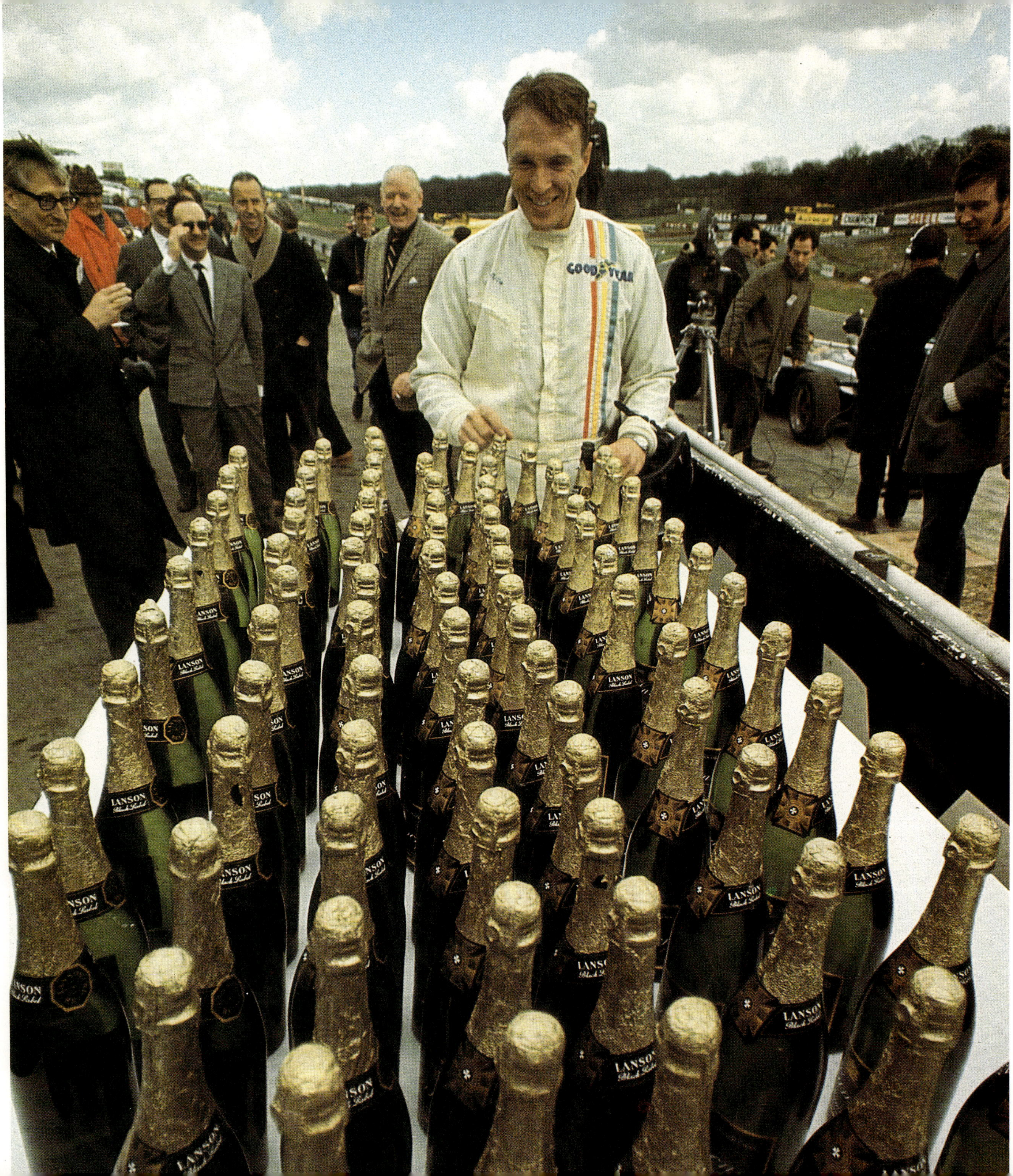
GOODYEAR
LANSON

1964, French Grand Prix, Rouen. Dan Gurney after his win in a Brabham.

Left: 1964, British Grand Prix, Brands Hatch. Dan won all this champagne for the fastest practice lap.

Right: 1964, US Grand Prix, Watkins Glen. Dan listens to a few words of advice from his boss, Jack Brabham.

following year Graham Hill and BRM won the championships. To make matters worse, at the end of 1962, Porsche pulled out of Formula One racing.

Dan then went to join the newly-formed Brabham team. A car was specially made for him to accommodate his 6 ft 3 in (1.90m) frame, although today he would be considered too tall to drive in Formula One. He had a moderately successful season scoring championship points in five of the ten Grands Prix.

Success came in 1964. Dan won two Grands Prix —the French, again at Rouen, and the Mexican. As he didn't have another win during the following year, however, Dan decided to leave Brabham and form his own Grand Prix racing team. After many discussions with Aubrey Woods, whom he had met at BRM, and Harry Weslake, it was decided to produce the Weslake-Gurney V12 and in the meantime to use a Coventry-Climax 4-cylinder engine in the Eagle, which was to be the name of his new car. Once again, it seems as though he chose the wrong time to make a move. In 1966, Brabham won the world championship, while Dan, in the Eagle-Climax, had to be satisfied with only two fifth places, at Reims and at Mexico City.

But the next year brought victories. At the beginning of the season, he won the Race of Champions at Brands Hatch in his beautiful shark-nosed Eagle, the work of Len Terry and Tony Southgate. Then, in one glorious June week, he and A. J. Foyt won Le Mans in a Ford Mk IV and Dan went on to win the Belgian Grand Prix in his own dark blue car by over a minute from Jackie Stewart in a BRM.

But that race was to be the swansong of Dan's driving career in Europe. Although he competed in a few Grands Prix for McLaren in 1970, he threw his energies into racing his own cars on the American

1967, Le Mans. Dan Gurney watches the champagne cork fly after his superb victory with A. J. Foyt. Driving their 7-litre Ford, the Americans had a race-long battle with the Ferrari P4 driven by Mike Parkes and Ludovico Scarfiotti, who finished second and who are also seen in this photograph.

Right: 1967, Belgian Grand Prix, Spa. Dan on his way to a magnificent victory in his own Eagle-Weslake.

1966, Indianapolis. Dan Gurney's Eagle.

circuits. In both 1967 and 1969, he came second in the Indianapolis 500. He retired at the end of 1970 but, in other hands, his Eagle cars were winners at Indianapolis in 1973 and 1975, and the Eagles are still leading competitors in sports car races.

Dan Gurney's magnetic personality made a great contribution to Formula One racing. Always good company, he loved champagne and would converse passionately and at length about cars and motorcycles. He would speak of his family with the same exuberance.

On the track, though his time in Formuala One was ultimately frustrating for him, Dan was a most aggressive and talented driver. He also loved tinkering with motor cars. It was this enthusiasm that led him to create his own team, which meant—and this I understand from my own experience—that he sometimes didn't get things quite right. Nevertheless, he was held in high esteem by all his fellow-drivers, and was always a great competitor.

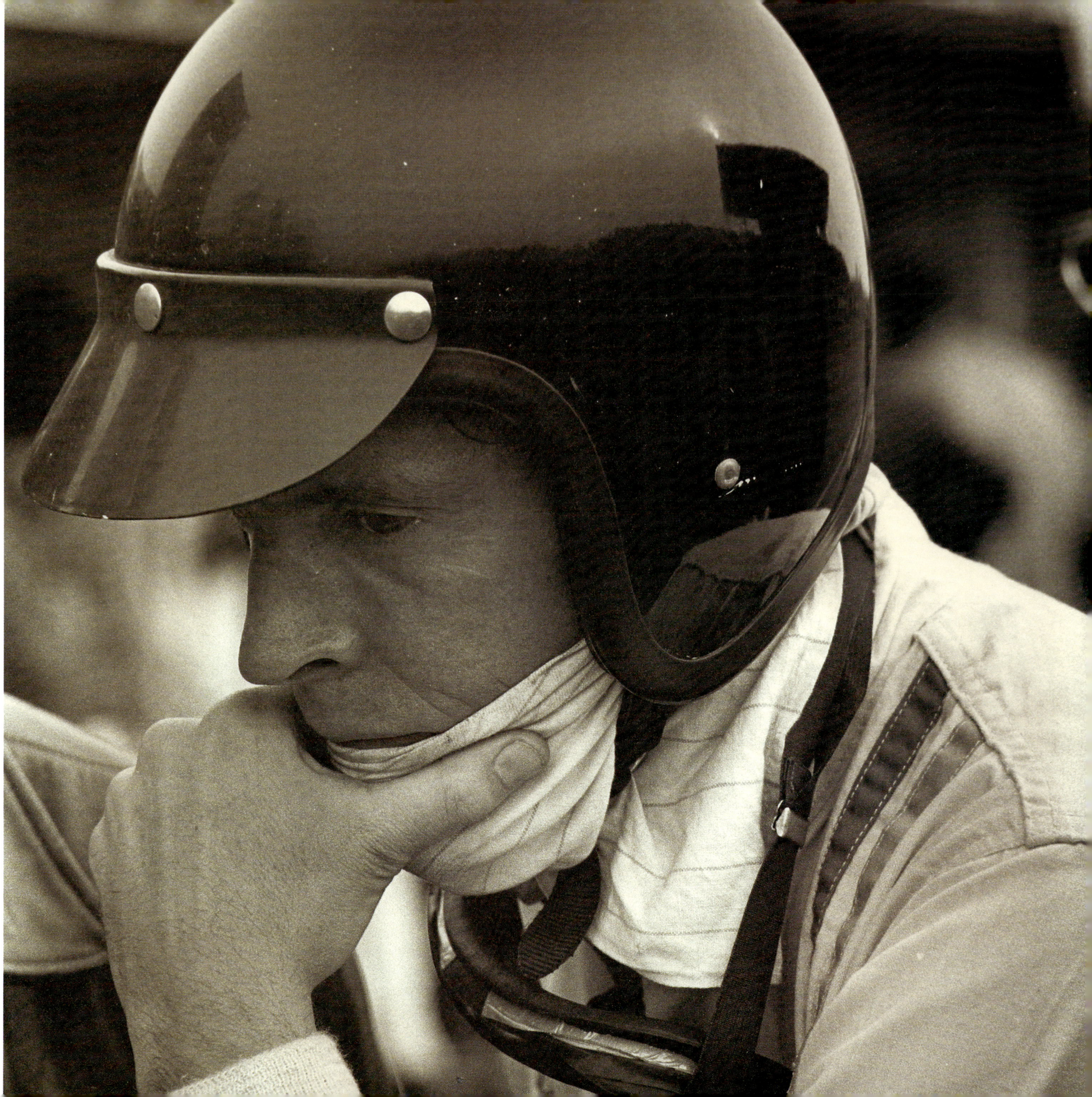

PIRELLI ALBUM OF MOTOR RACING HEROES

MIKE HAILWOOD

After winning almost everything he could on two wheels, Mike Hailwood took up motor racing. He never scored a Formula One victory, but his aggressive style of driving and his courageous rescue of Regazzoni from a blazing BRM during the 1973 South African Grand Prix brought him great popular acclaim.

1963, Ulster Grand Prix, Belfast. Minister's wife Mrs Craig congratulates Mike Hailwood on his win.

Far right: June 1967, Senior TT, Isle of Man. Mike on his way to victory at Douglas at a record average speed of 105.62 mph.

For Mike Hailwood, competing was a way of life. In some quarters he gained a reputation as a hell-raiser. Certainly he wasn't abstemious and didn't tuck himself into bed at nine o'clock the night before a race. But he was never careless about the job in hand. He was fully aware of the risks and the moment the flag dropped would become a highly skilled and competitive driver.

'Racing is a sickness with us,' he once said. 'I can't start to explain it. But once a race starts, nothing matters except driving. I may be the least dedicated sportsman in the world. But I've had an urge to do something and what I've gained from it, apart from the excitement, is the feeling that I've achieved something extraordinary.'

Even though Mike was six years my junior, in a way we grew up together. His father and mine were both motorcycle dealers and raced motorcycle sidecars against each other on grass tracks before the war.

In 1957, when he was 17, Mike started racing on a 250 cc NSU Sportmax I'd lent him—the bike I'd ridden in the 1955 Ulster Grand Prix to score my first world

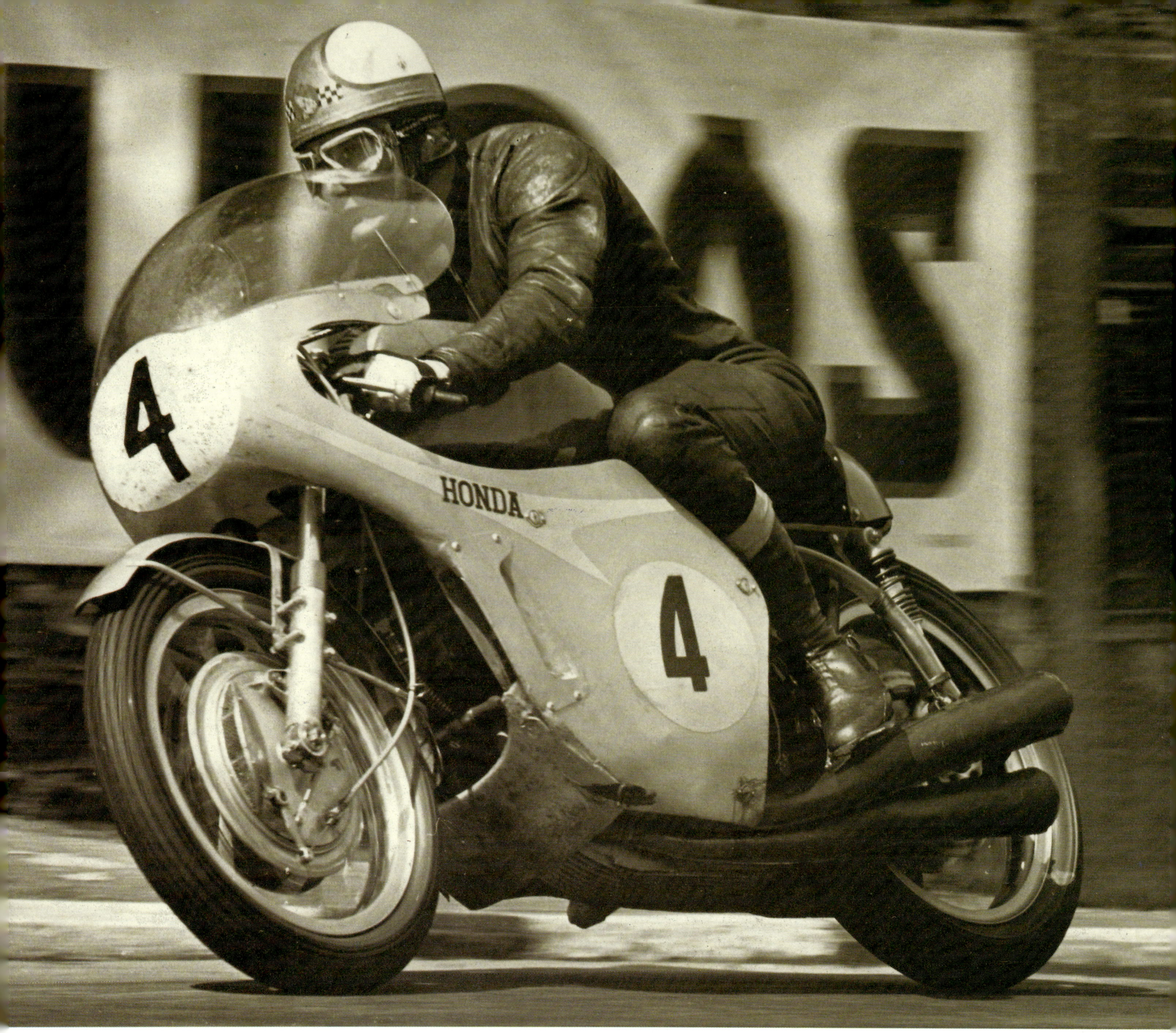
4
HONDA
4

Brooke Bond Oxo
Rob Walker
BUCKHAMS
10
Brooke Bond Oxo
Rob Walker
Firestone
10
BUCKHAMS
BUCKHAMS
SURTEES

MIKE HAILWOOD

Brands Hatch. Two wheels and four—Mike on a Honda and (left) in a Team Surtees F1 car.

1973, South African Grand Prix, Kyalami. (Top right) Hailwood racing the Surtees before Regazzoni's fiery accident in the BRM and (right) silhouetted against the blaze.

championship victory. By the time Mike decided, in the late sixties, to retire and concentrate on motor car racing, he had won nine motorcycling world championships and a record 12 Isle of Man TT races.

By then, I'd started my own racing team and had developed a successful Formula 5000 car, the Surtees TS5. I'd watched Mike driving against us in a Lola T190. It wasn't the best of cars and, although many people remarked that Mike was a little crazy as a driver, it was obvious that he was able and very fast.

So I said to him, 'Mike, I think I understand many of the problems faced by a motorcyclist coming into cars. Let's get together. We'll make a good team.'

Mike was a very straightforward, honest person. We just talked things over and then shook hands. It wasn't necessary to have a written agreement with him.

In his first season with us, he drove our Formula 5000 car with considerable success. Then, in September 1971, he had his first Formula One outing in a Surtees-Ford, finishing fourth by less than a second in the Italian Grand Prix at Monza. The following year, 1972,

1974. Mike Hailwood had moved to Yardley McLaren at the end of the previous year. Team Surtees was sad to see him go. Shortage of money at the time, as so often in motor racing, was the reason.

'Racing is a sickness with us,' Mike Hailwood once said. 'I can't start to explain it. But once a race starts, nothing matters except driving. I may be the least dedicated sportsman in the world but I've had an urge to do something and what I've gained from it, apart from the excitement, is the feeling that I've achieved something extraordinary.'

he won the European Formula Two championship in the Team Surtees TS10 car and had several impressive Formula One outings, including the Italian Grand Prix where Emerson Fittipaldi beat him to first place by a split second.

Mike stayed with Team Surtees for 1973 and early that year he displayed great courage in saving the life of a fellow driver. During the South African Grand Prix at Kyalami, Dave Charlton lost control of his Lotus under braking for Crowthorne Corner and Mike in the Surtees was unable to avoid him. Jacky Ickx (Ferrari) and Clay Regazzoni (BRM) struck Mike's car, the BRM's monocoque split open and the car burst into flames, setting the Surtees alight, too. Mike was able to leap out, but Regazzoni was slumped unconscious in his blazing cockpit. The marshals—some in shorts, some in safari suits— made only tentative attempts to fight the fire and rescue the BRM driver.

Not so Mike Hailwood, who without hesitation leapt into the flames and succeeded in releasing Regazzoni's safety harness. But his overalls and gloves caught fire and, beaten back by the intense heat, he was unable to drag the still unconscious Regazzoni from the car. When the marshals finally managed to douse the blaze a little, Mike courageously returned to the crumpled wreck and pulled Regazzoni to safety. Only then

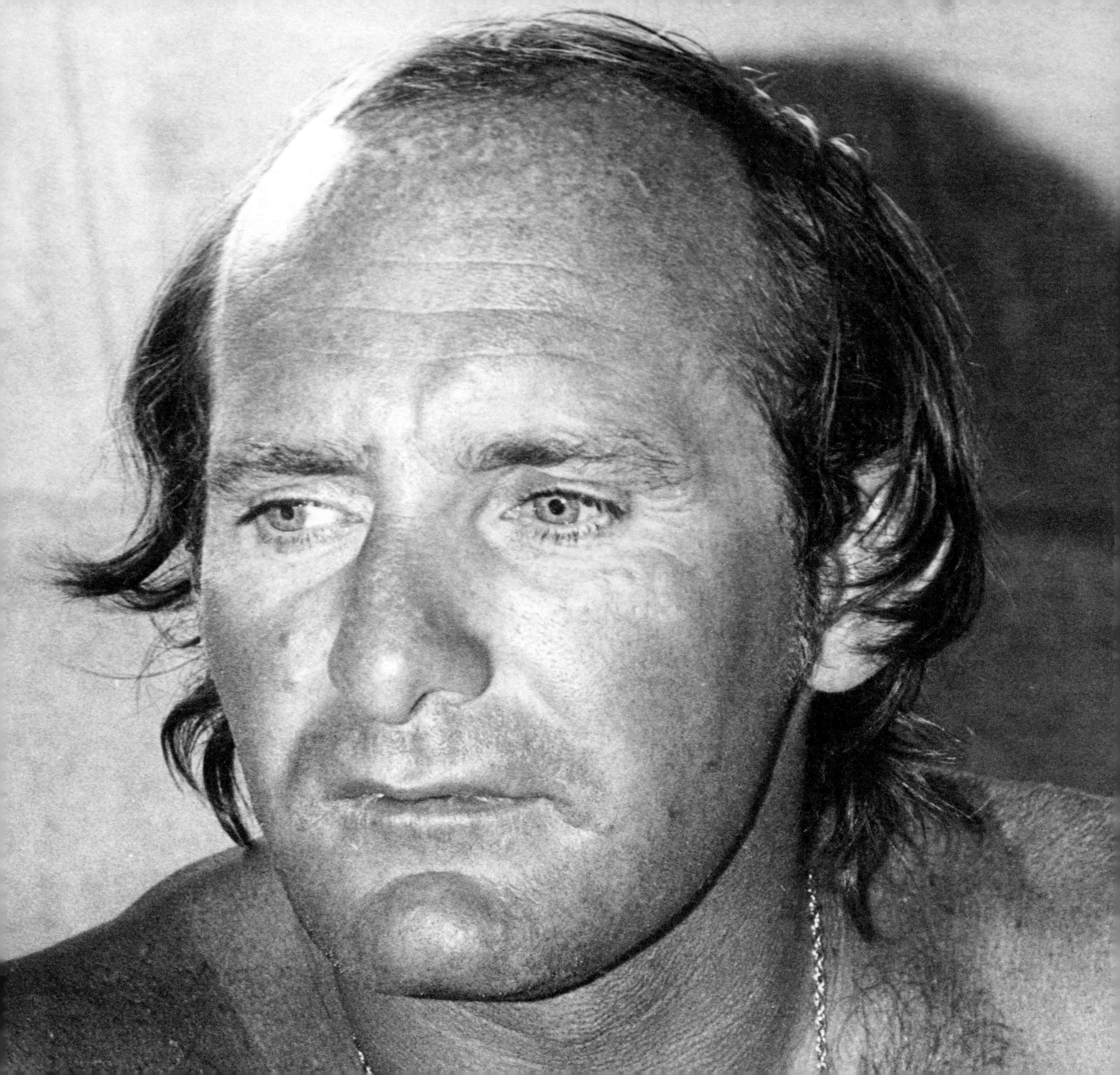

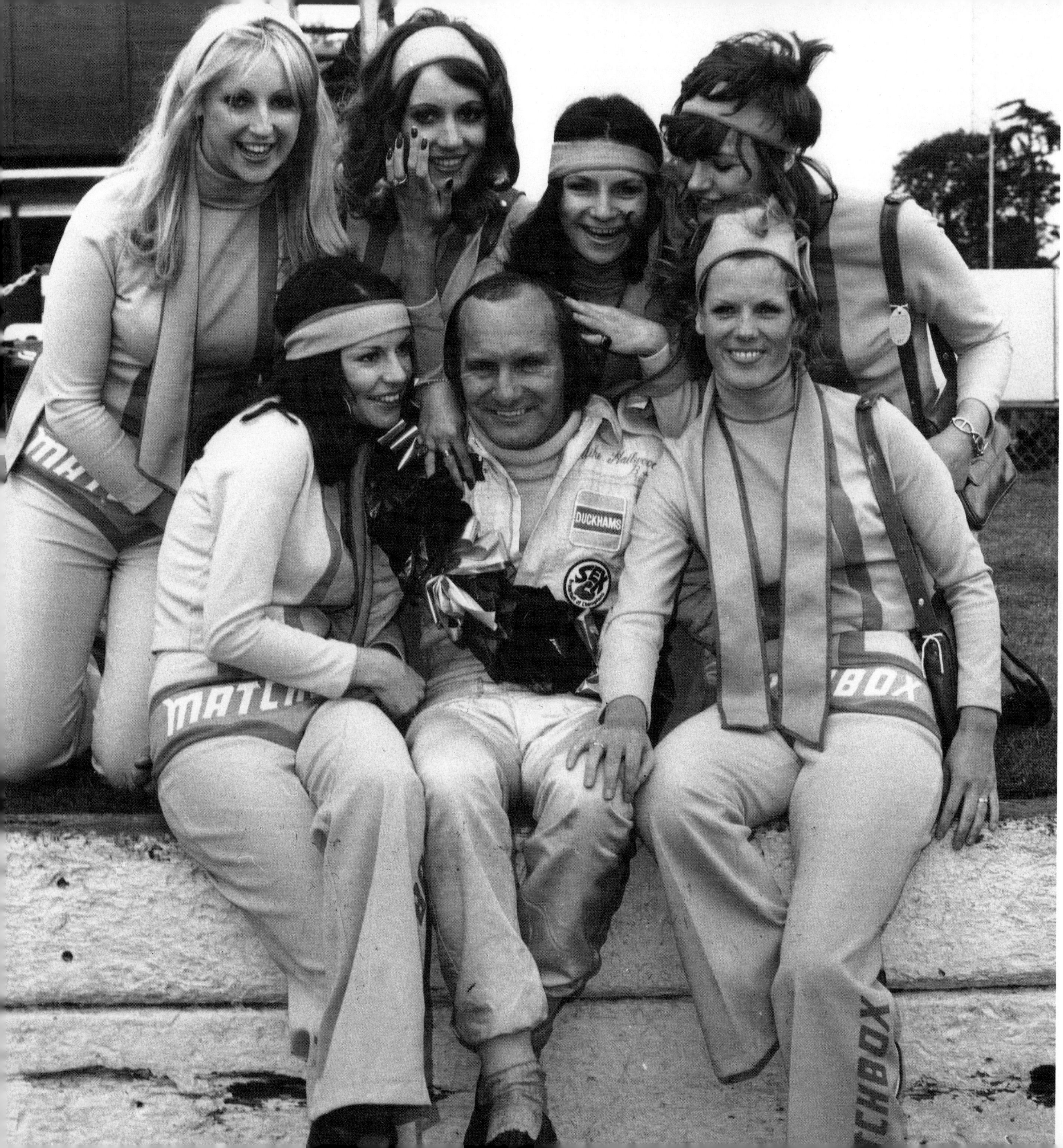
DUCKHAMS

MIKE HAILWOOD

Mike Hailwood with James Hunt on a Honda.

Above right: 6 August 1978, Silverstone. Mike makes his farewell appearance.

Right: Two years later, he was non-riding captain of the British team in the Transatlantic Trophy races.

Left: Mike at Team Surtees. Matchbox, a Team Surtees sponsor, supplied the girls!

did Kyalami's brand-new, high-speed fire engine and an ambulance arrive on the scene.

The Swiss driver was lucky to get away with only minor burns to his hands and without doubt he owed his life to Mike. For his selfless and courageous action Hailwood was later awarded the George Cross, Britain's highest civil award for bravery.

At the end of 1973, with no money in the kitty, Team Surtees reluctantly had to let Mike go and he moved to Yardley McLaren. He seemed set for a good season, finishing fourth in Argentina, fifth in Brazil and third in South Africa. He was fourth again in Holland, but his promising career came to a painful end at the Nürburgring six weeks later. He had a big accident in practice when the McLaren's front suspension failed. He was able to walk away unharmed, but during the Grand Prix he crashed again, very heavily, and this time he did not walk away. His left foot was badly crushed, leaving him with very restricted ankle movement and sadly that was the end of his motor racing career.

In 1978, however, eleven years after giving up competitive motorcycling, Mike returned to the Isle of Man and won his 14th TT! He retired in 1979 after 21 years of racing.

Two years later, during a torrential May downpour, he and his nine-year-old daughter were killed when the Rover 3500 saloon he was driving ran into an unlit lorry which was crossing the central reservation of a dual carriageway a few miles from his home.

101

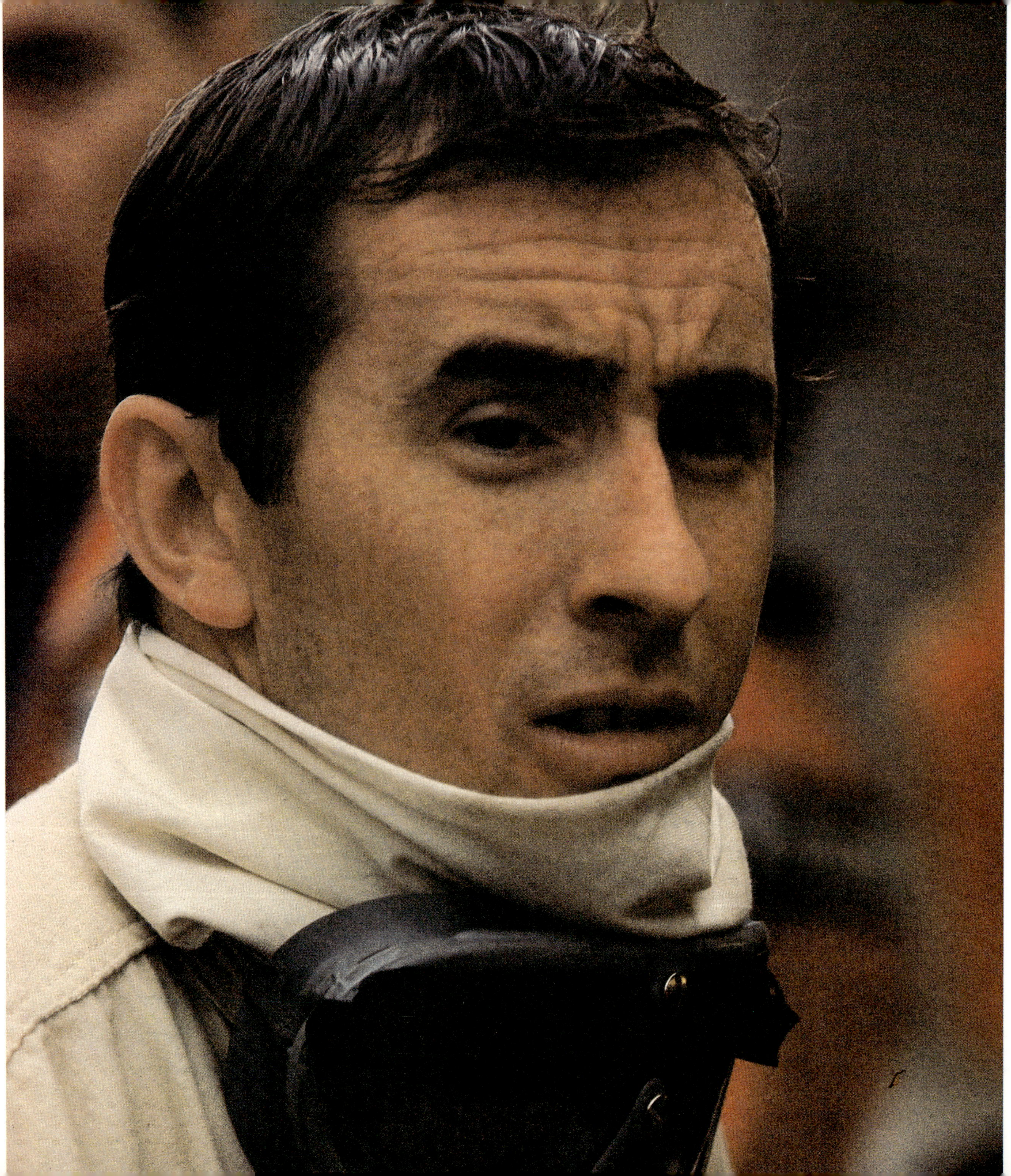

JACKIE STEWART

It could be said that Jackie Stewart followed in the footsteps of Jim Clark. Built rather like Jim, small and lean, but more intense and visibly self-confident, Stewart also has had two extraordinarily successful careers. Jim led parallel lives on and off the track, but Stewart's racing career with its three world championships was followed by an equally successful one as an ex-driver.

1966, Indianapolis 500. Stewart came agonisingly close to victory in his first attempt at the Indy.

In 1966, a year after winning his first Grand Prix, Jackie Stewart was asked what qualities a driver needed to become world champion. 'First, he must be a hungry driver,' Stewart replied. 'I am a hungry driver. I want the best the life can offer me. Of course it is speed that wins races. But a champion will always win his races as slowly as he can. Driving perfection, not recklessness, wins races consistently.'

In the years that followed, Stewart applied all his natural dedication, shrewdness and meticulousness to ensuring that racing brought him significant social and financial rewards.

Many people, including some of his racing colleagues, questioned whether he had a real love of motor sport. It was the kind of comment that Stewart dismissed scornfully.

'Infatuation is one of the evils of the world,' he declared, 'whether it's for a woman or a sport. I race because it's the one thing I can do better than anything else.' And he was successful. Between 1968 and 1973, when he retired at 34, he was a leading Grand Prix driver, winning the world championship three times. Throughout that period he drove for Ken Tyrrell, who, through his own Grand Prix team, has made such

1965, Italian Grand Prix, Monza. This race saw Stewart's first Grand Prix win, for BRM.

4 August 1968, German Grand Prix, Nürburgring. Jackie Stewart's most famous race, through thickening fog and torrential rain, which he won over four minutes ahead of Graham Hill.

a significant contribution to motor racing.

During those years, Stewart was as much a driving force off the track as he was on it. He became a dominant advocate of new safety measures in the Grand Prix Drivers' Association after he'd crashed in the 1966 Belgian Grand Prix at Spa.

In heavy rain, during the first lap of the Belgian race, his BRM flew off the track, struck a telegraph pole and demolished a woodcutter's hut. The car was leaking petrol and Stewart was trapped behind his steering wheel in the wreckage. Graham Hill and Bob Bondurant, whose cars had spun off nearby, tried to rescue him, but it took 25 minutes before they were able to release the Scot, using tools found in the back of a spectator's car. As an ambulance still hadn't arrived, Stewart was laid in the back of a van.

Five minutes later, an ambulance reached the scene and took him to the first aid station near the control tower. As it was feared his spine might be injured, he was left to lie on the stretcher. At last it was decided he should be taken to Liège, but incredibly the police escort managed to lose its way.

Finally, Stewart was taken to an airport and flown to St Thomas's Hospital, London, where he was relieved to learn he was suffering from nothing worse

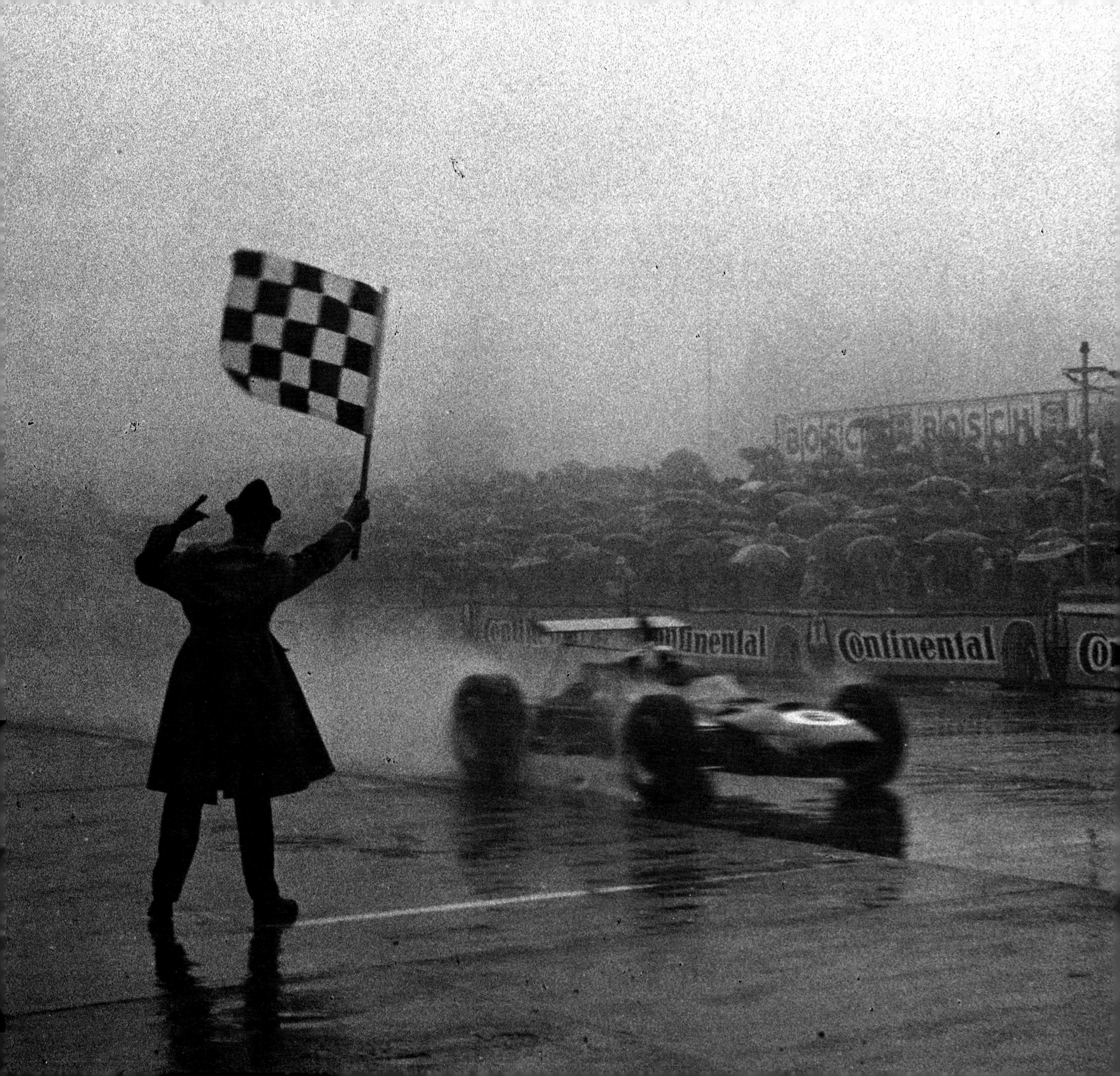
Continental

A victorious Stewart and his wife Helen with Prince Rainier and Princess Grace of Monaco.

1974. Jackie Stewart in the Tyrrell-Ford. Note the Stewart or 'Royal' tartan adorning his helmet.

Right: 1973. Stewart with his mentor Ken Tyrrell, the wealthy Surrey timber merchant who has made such a great contribution to Formula One racing.

Jackie Stewart was angrily outspoken about the way the sport seemed to accept the deaths of racing drivers—but only off the track. When racing, he was entirely self-controlled. 'When I get into the car,' he once said, 'there's no emotion in me—none at all. There's no nerves when the man raises the flag, nothing.'

Right: 1971, Monaco Grand Prix. Stewart enters the tunnel in his Tyrrell, 003.

than a split bone beneath the pelvis, three broken ribs and a smashed collar-bone. From then on, his BRM always had a spanner taped inside the cockpit in case the steering wheel needed to be removed swiftly!

Afterwards, Stewart threw his considerable organizational abilities into demanding, with others, that race tracks should be made safer and be properly staffed with trained marshals and top-class medical teams. Such measures were long overdue. Between 1966 and 1973, no fewer than 57 drivers were killed in Grand Prix and sports car racing. They included Jim Clark, Bruce McLaren, Piers Courage and Jochen Rindt. Many improvements had, of course, already been made. Bag tanks and monocoque construction meant that in an accident the car should neither catch fire, nor blow up around the driver capsule. After the Belgian GP, Stewart's voice was clamorous for track safety measures, and most circuits then sported guard rails—a feature that to my mind remains a dubious advantage.

Stewart's calmness, calculation and confidence were most clearly demonstrated during the German Grand Prix held at the Nürburgring on 4 August 1968. The weather was treacherous with incessant rain and dense fog rolling down from the peaks of the Eifel mountains. Stewart, at the wheel of the Tyrrell team's blue V8 Matra-Ford, had his right wrist encased in a

1973, Dutch Grand Prix, Zandvoort. Stewart driving a Tyrrell-Ford.

1973, British Grand Prix, Silverstone. Jackie Stewart shortly before the race.

Far right: Jackie Stewart with his son Paul at their home in Switzerland.

plastic brace, the result of an accident four months earlier. As the flag came down, Jackie shot through on the inside from the third row and tucked in behind Graham Hill's Lotus.

By the end of the first lap of the 22.8 km (14.2 mile) mountain circuit with its 173 corners, Stewart emerged through the fog as the leader by 8.2 seconds. By the end of the second of the 14 laps, as the fog thickened, his lead had been extended to 47 seconds. At the half-way stage, he was one and a half minutes ahead!

The last lap saw the pits awash, the cars throwing up plumes of spray, and an unruffled Jackie Stewart burst through the blanket of fog to take the chequered flag—with a drenched crowd of 200,000 on their feet—over four minutes ahead of Hill in second place.

It was only his third Grand Prix win. But, that day, Stewart, a born performer, stepped into the limelight. He's rarely been out of it since.

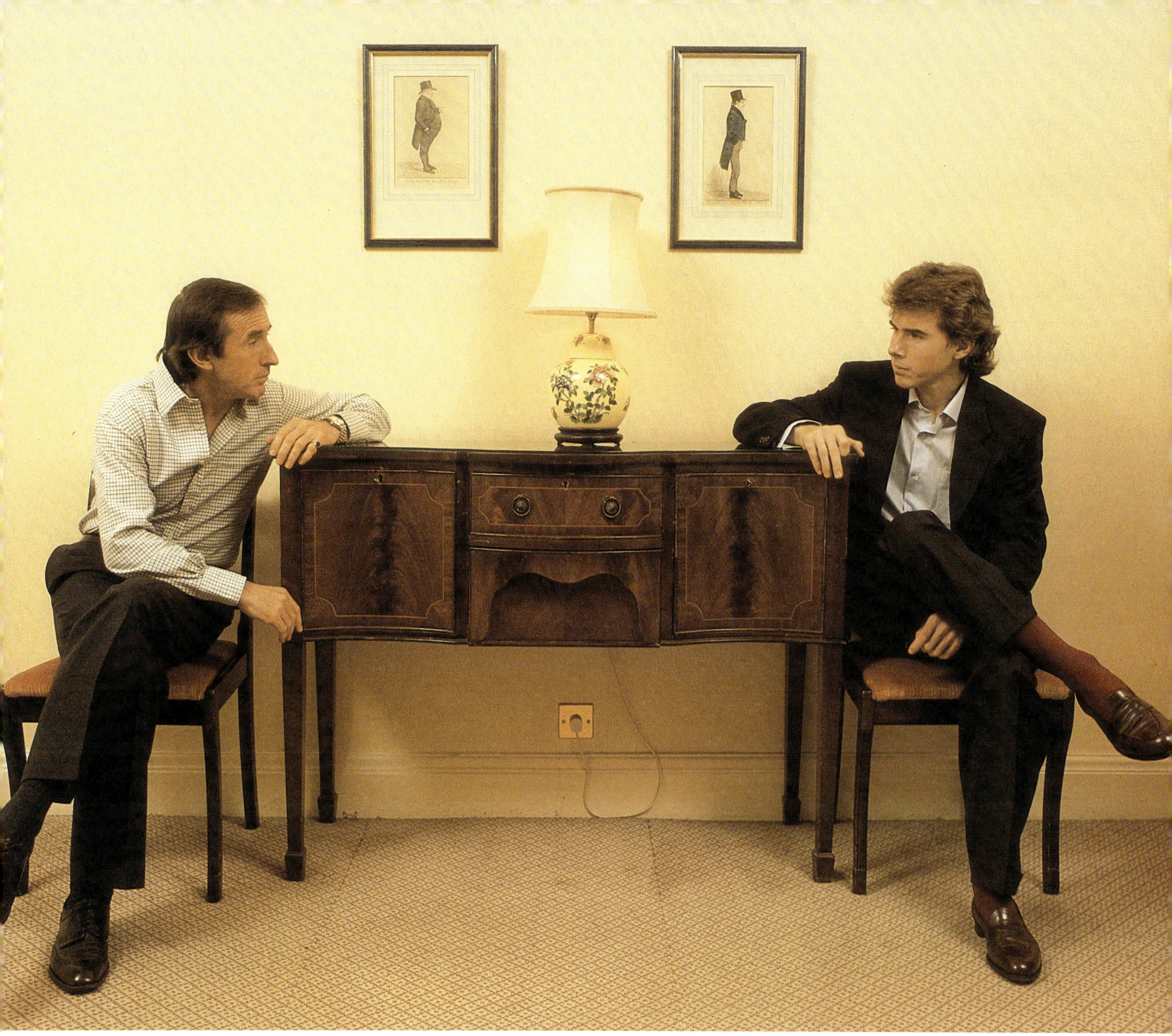

MARIO ANDRETTI

Known for his charm off the track and his complete driving skills on it, Mario Andretti epitomizes the American dream. An Italian immigrant who arrived in the United States unable to speak English, he became his adopted country's most successful Formula One driver, an Indianapolis 500 winner, and a CART champion.

1968, US Grand Prix, Watkins Glen. Mario Andretti won pole position for his very first Grand Prix.

Far right: May 1965, Mario Andretti at Indianapolis.

I cannot help feeling that Mario has been around for ever. Now over fifty, he's still a brilliant racing driver. Although a Wall Street stockbroker and owner of a chain of Italian restaurants across the United States, I can confirm that his real interest has always been racing any car that could be raced. I've driven against him many times, not only in Formula One but in many different makes of sports cars.

Mario was born in Montona, near Trieste, in an area of Italy that, soon after the war, became part of Yugoslavia. He and his family then spent some years interned in a displaced persons' camp before emigrating to the United States. They settled in Nazareth, Pennsylvania, which Mario came to love so much that he lives there still.

He soon started his racing career in America and victories quickly followed. Between 1965 and 1969, he won the US Auto Club National Championship three

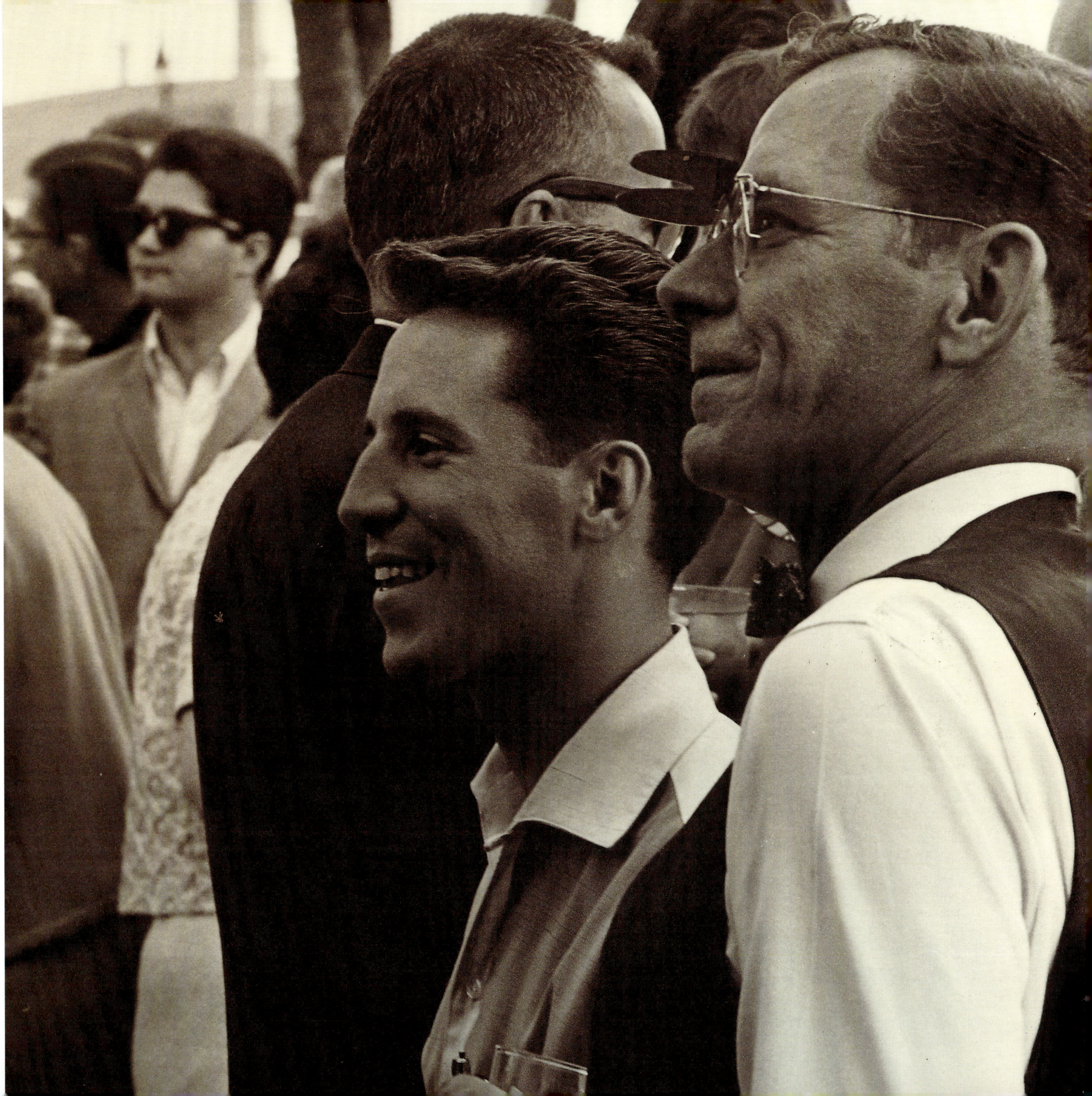

MARIO ANDRETTI

Left: 1977, US Grand Prix, Long Beach. Andretti in the Lotus 78 during the first US Grand Prix to be held in California.

Above Right: 1976, Japanese Grand Prix, Fuji. Andretti in the Lotus leads the field at the start. He went on to win.

Right: 1978, Dutch Grand Prix, Zandvoort. Andretti leads Lotus team-mate Ronnie Peterson.

times and was runner-up twice. In 1965, his rookie year, he came third behind two Lotus cars in the Indianapolis 500, a race he was to win in 1969.

His performance at Indy so impressed Colin Chapman of Lotus that he said he'd make a car available whenever Mario wanted to try Formula One. Towards the end of 1968, he took up the offer and I drove against him in his first outing—the United States Grand Prix at Watkins Glen. Mario captured pole position but after a few laps he was forced to retire with clutch trouble.

For the next two years, he had only occasional Formula One drives but, at the beginning of 1971, he received an offer he couldn't refuse—to drive for Ferrari whenever his American commitments allowed. He had a dream start to the season, winning his first race with Ferrari—the South African Grand Prix at Kyalami. Later, he finished fourth at the Nürburgring and was offered a permanent place in the Ferrari team —but he turned it down and returned to the United States. Ferrari was to summon him again, however.

He was back in Europe in 1974, driving for the Vels Parnelli racing operation, but the team enjoyed only limited success and was disbanded early in 1976. Mario then rejoined Colin Chapman, whose Team Lotus had just had its worst season for 16 years. Sam Moses of *Sports Illustrated* stated dismissively, 'Here's a has-been constructor getting together with a has-been driver.' He couldn't have been more wrong.

Chapman, who was not the easiest man to work for, had a great respect not only for Mario's driving ability and stamina but also for his clear perception of the fine tuning a car needed. Although they often had monumental arguments, the two men worked well together. Success came in the last race of the season—

the 1976 Japanese Grand Prix. This Formula One championship victory was the first for Lotus since September 1974 and Mario's first since March 1971.

For the 1977 season, Chapman produced his new Lotus 78. 'You wait until you see it,' Mario announced. 'It feels like it's painted to the road!'

A series of blown engines deprived Mario of the 1977 title, although he had more wins than any other driver. The first of his four successes came in April at Long Beach—no American had ever before won a United States Grand Prix. For much of the race, he was tucked in behind the leader, Jody Scheckter in his Wolf. 'I stayed so close to him,' Mario said, 'I could read the labels on his collar.' Three laps from the end, Mario swept by.

Later in 1977, he was delighted—as an Italian by birth—to win the Italian Grand Prix at Monza, and the exuberant crowd shared his joy. By the time he returned there the following year, he had already won six Grands Prix. His sixth place in the 1978 Italian GP ensured that he achieved his life's ambition to become the Formula One World Champion. But his triumph was tainted by tragedy. At the very start of the race, his Lotus team-mate and close friend Ronnie Peterson crashed. He died in hospital some twelve hours later.

This team tragedy disturbed Mario and, though there was never any question of his giving up motor sport, he became increasingly dissatisfied with the developments that were taking place in Formula One. After a couple of lack-lustre seasons, he announced he was giving up full-time Grand Prix racing to concentrate on re-establishing his career as an Indy Car driver.

It looked as though his racing days in Europe were over but then, in September 1982, he received a

1978, Monza. Mario with Colin Chapman.

In 1977, Andretti was delighted—as an Italian by birth—to win the Italian Grand Prix at Monza, and the exuberant crowd shared his joy. By the time he returned there the following year, he had already won six Grands Prix. His sixth place in the 1978 Italian GP ensured that he achieved his life's ambition to become the Formula One World Champion.

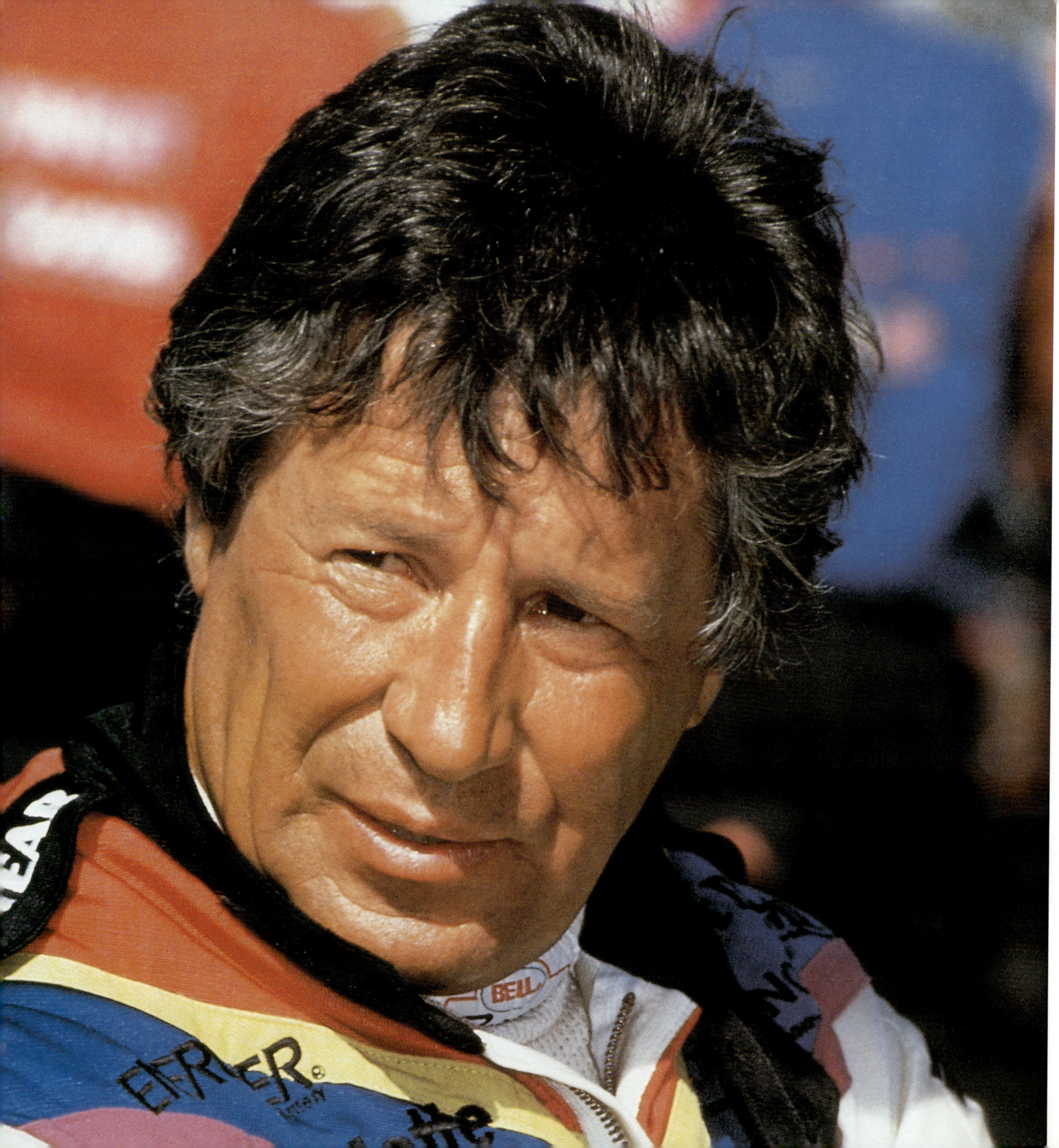
BELL

MARIO ANDRETTI

Left: 1991 CART season. Mario Andretti.

call from Enzo Ferrari. With Didier Pironi injured, he needed a driver to partner Patrick Tambay in the Italian Grand Prix at Monza. 'A Ferrari at Monza!' Mario exclaimed. 'How does a guy say no to that?'

His arrival at Malpensa Airport was shown live on Italian television and, to the delight of all Italy, when Mario emerged from the aircraft, he was already wearing a Ferrari cap. Nor did he let down the excited crowd at the race. He started in pole position and finished his last Grand Prix drive in fourth place.

Afterwards, he went back to CART racing, winning in 1984 the championship he'd last held in 1969. He is still racing and, as the founder of the Andretti dynasty of famed American drivers, he faces the unique challenge of competing regularly against his sons, Michael and Jeff, and his nephew, John.

Mario Andretti and son Michael, team-mates at Le Mans.

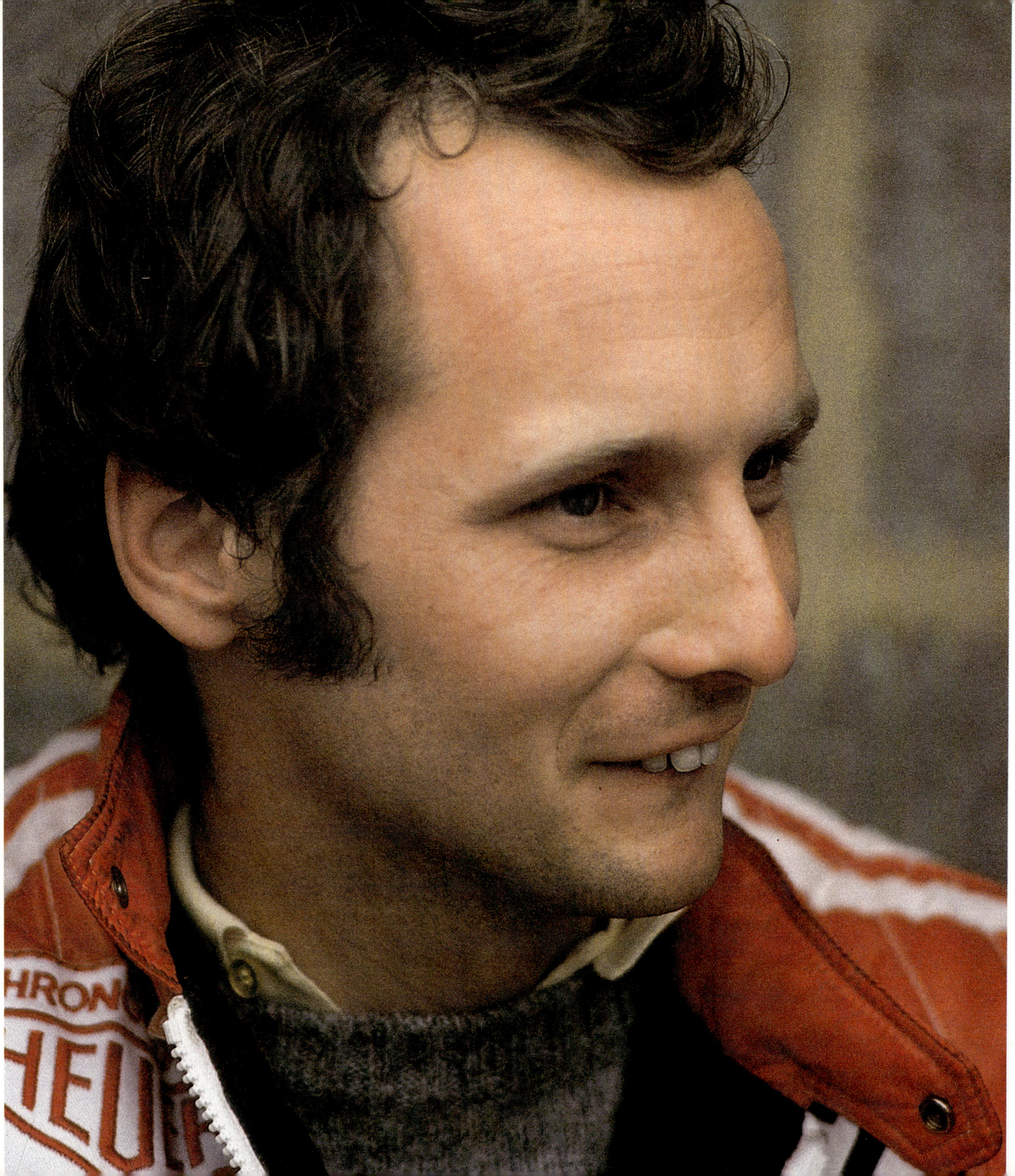

NIKI LAUDA

It was thought that Niki Lauda, the reigning world champion, was unlikely to live after his Ferrari crashed and burst into flames at the old Nürburgring on 1 August 1976. Six weeks later, his facial burns barely healed, he astonished the world by successfully resuming his racing career.

Above right: 1974, Spanish Grand Prix, Jarama. Lauda scoring his first Grand Prix victory for Ferrari.

Right: 1975, French Grand Prix, Le Castelet. Champagne, laurels and adulation for Niki Lauda after his victory for Ferrari. James Hunt also seems pleased with his second place in the Hesketh-Ford.

Nicklaus Andreas Lauda was only 19 when he competed in his first races, driving a Mini Cooper. Three years later, in 1971, he borrowed £30,000 to buy a one-off Formula One Grand Prix drive in a March 711.

His Austrian debut wasn't impressive but he was determined to succeed and I even had some discussions with him about driving for Team Surtees, but nothing came of them. In 1972, he won the British Formula Two championship. The following season, he became the number three driver, to Jean-Pierre Beltoise and Clay Regazzoni, in the BRM Formula One team.

The BRM P160 wasn't a very competitive car, but Lauda had some fine, if sometimes short-lived, drives. His best result was in Belgium where he came fifth. In the British Grand Prix at Silverstone, he lay second for a while and fought hard to stay in the leading group. It was a determined, calculated performance.

Clay Regazzoni was so impressed that, when he returned to Ferrari after his year's interval with BRM, he suggested to Enzo Ferrari that Lauda should be brought into the team. Ferrari took Regazzoni's advice and Lauda instantly revealed his self-confidence and mechanical acumen. In his first Grand Prix of 1974, he came second and went on to win both the Spanish and Dutch Grands Prix.

NIKI LAUDA

1975, Monaco Grand Prix. Lauda wins in the single Ferrari 312 left in the race after team-mate Regazzoni's accident.

In 1975, with five victories, he ran away with the world championship. For much of the 1976 season, Lauda seemed certain to repeat his previous year's triumph. He won five of the first nine races and was 14 championship points ahead of James Hunt.

Then came the German Grand Prix. A week before, Lauda had stated, 'Nürburgring is too dangerous to drive on nowadays. If you have any car failure, it is 100 per cent death.' Fortunately for him, he was wrong.

During the second lap of the race, Lauda's Ferrari hurtled through the safety fence, hit a bank and, as it shot back onto the track, burst into flames. Brett Lunger, in one of my Team Surtees cars, braked hard but clipped the wreckage which was then rammed by Harald Ertl in a Hesketh. Following close behind were Guy Edwards and Arturo Merzario, who both managed to stop without incident.

Far right: 1976, Japanese Grand Prix, Fuji. Lauda's decision to retire was a consummate act of courage. In appalling conditions, James Hunt came fourth in his McLaren-Ford to score enough points to become the season's champion.

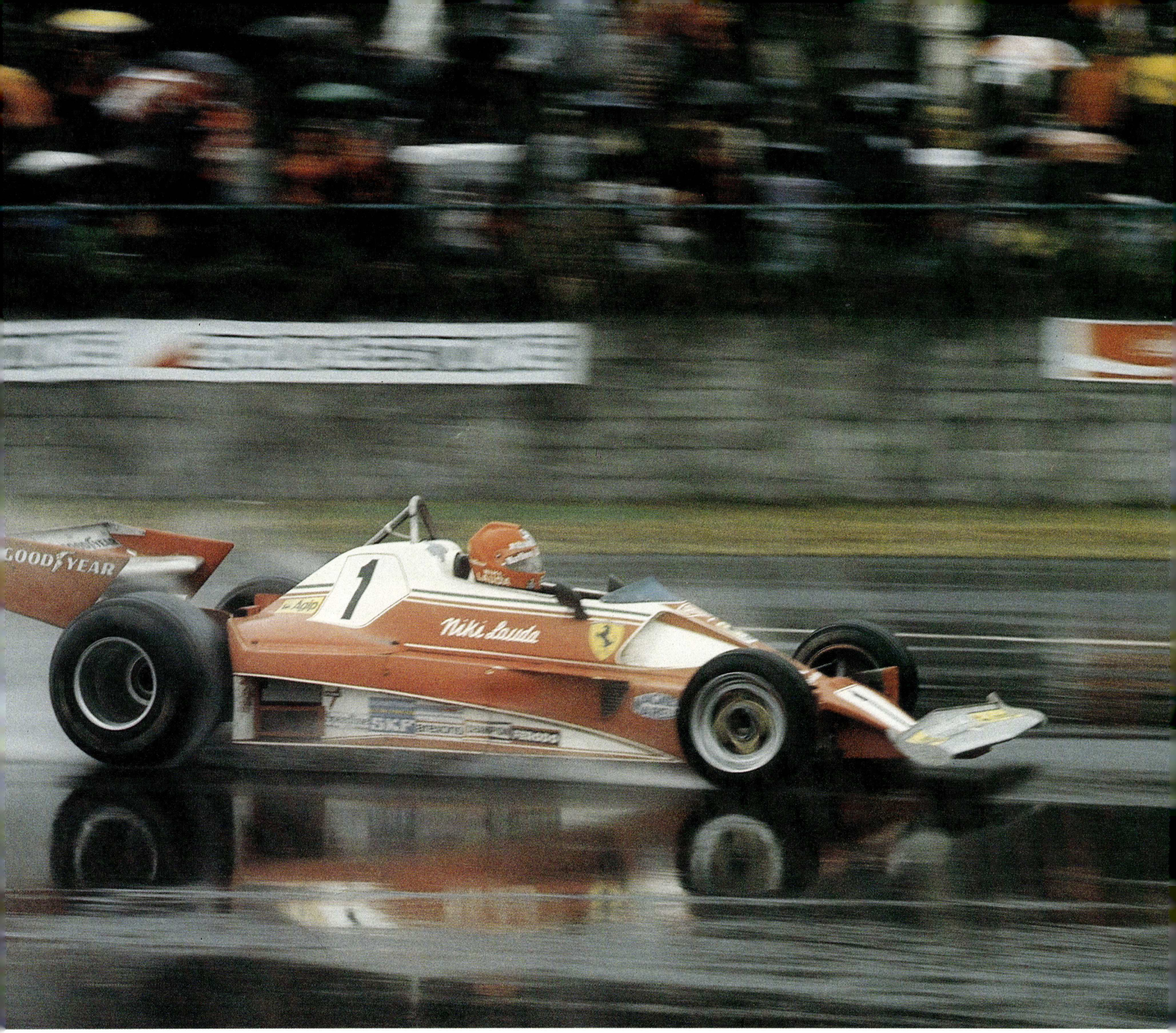
GOODYEAR
1
Niki Lauda

NIKI LAUDA

NIKI LAUDA

Left: Niki Lauda fought hard to establish Lauda Air and build it into a successful airline.

Right: Lauda deep in conversation, wearing the world-famous red Parmalat cap.

In 1975, with five victories, Lauda ran away with the world championship. For much of the 1976 season, he seemed certain to repeat his previous year's triumph. He won five of the first nine races and was 14 championship points ahead of James Hunt.

It is on record that Lunger, Edwards, Ertl and Merzario rushed bravely towards the inferno. As the fire was so intense, Ertl sprinted back to his car to collect a fire-extinguisher with which he kept down the flames as Lunger clambered onto the back of the Ferrari while Merzario on one side and Edwards on the other tried to rescue Lauda who was unconscious and ablaze. Somehow or other in the crash, he'd lost his helmet and his protective balaclava was blackening in the heat.

It took over a minute to undo the safety belts, heave him out and drag him off the track. It took another agonizing minute to subdue the fire that enveloped him. It was a further nine minutes before an ambulance arrived on the scene.

Suffering from seared lungs and extensive burns to his head and hands, Lauda was rushed to hospital and placed in intensive care. For four days, he was on the brink of death and indeed received the last rites. But he fought desperately to live and slowly began to recover.

At Monza, 41 days after the accident, Lauda was racing a Ferrari, finishing fourth in the Italian Grand Prix even though his wounds were by no means healed.

Before the last Grand Prix of the season, Lauda still led the championship three points ahead of Hunt. Race day was grey and wet. Heavy rain had left vast lakes on much of the track. Conditions were so bad that most drivers were unwilling to compete but, after much debate and delay, the Japanese Grand Prix at last began.

After the second lap Lauda drove into the pits and

123

NIKI LAUDA

1985, British Grand Prix, Silverstone. Lauda strapped into the cockpit of his McLaren-TAG before the start. He is talking to Barry Sheene, former motorcycle world champion.

1984, British Grand Prix, Brands Hatch. Getting there... Lauda powering the McLaren-TAG to victory and throwing in the fastest lap for good measure.

Far right: 1984, South African Grand Prix, Kyalami. Niki Lauda and Alain Prost sunning themselves at the poolside before their 1-2 success for McLaren-TAG.

announced he was pulling out of the race because the weather conditions made it too dangerous to continue. Many cars spun off the track that afternoon, but Hunt finished and, by coming third, collected sufficient points to overtake Lauda's total and become the 1976 world champion.

At the time, many people, especially in Italy, found Lauda's decision incomprehensible. As I see it now, in retrospect, it was a brave decision on the part of a man whose personal courage was unquestionable.

Having demonstrated his fierce independence, Lauda went on, in 1977, to win his second world championship. He then left Ferrari to join the Brabham team. Almost at the end of his second season with them, he unexpectedly announced his retirement. Two years later, in 1982, he returned to drive for McLaren. In 1984, he won his third world championship by half a point from his team-mate Alain Prost. The following season, he finally retired for good to concentrate on his business interests, especially the successful development of his airline, Lauda Air. In February 1992, he returned to Ferrari—this time as a consultant.

This remarkable man is rightly celebrated not so much for his many racing victories as for the outstanding way in which, after his horrendous accident, he fought not just to hold on to life but to regain full fitness and re-establish himself at the top of Formula One. Furthermore, his enterprise off the track and attractive personality ensure that Lauda's name will not be forgotten.

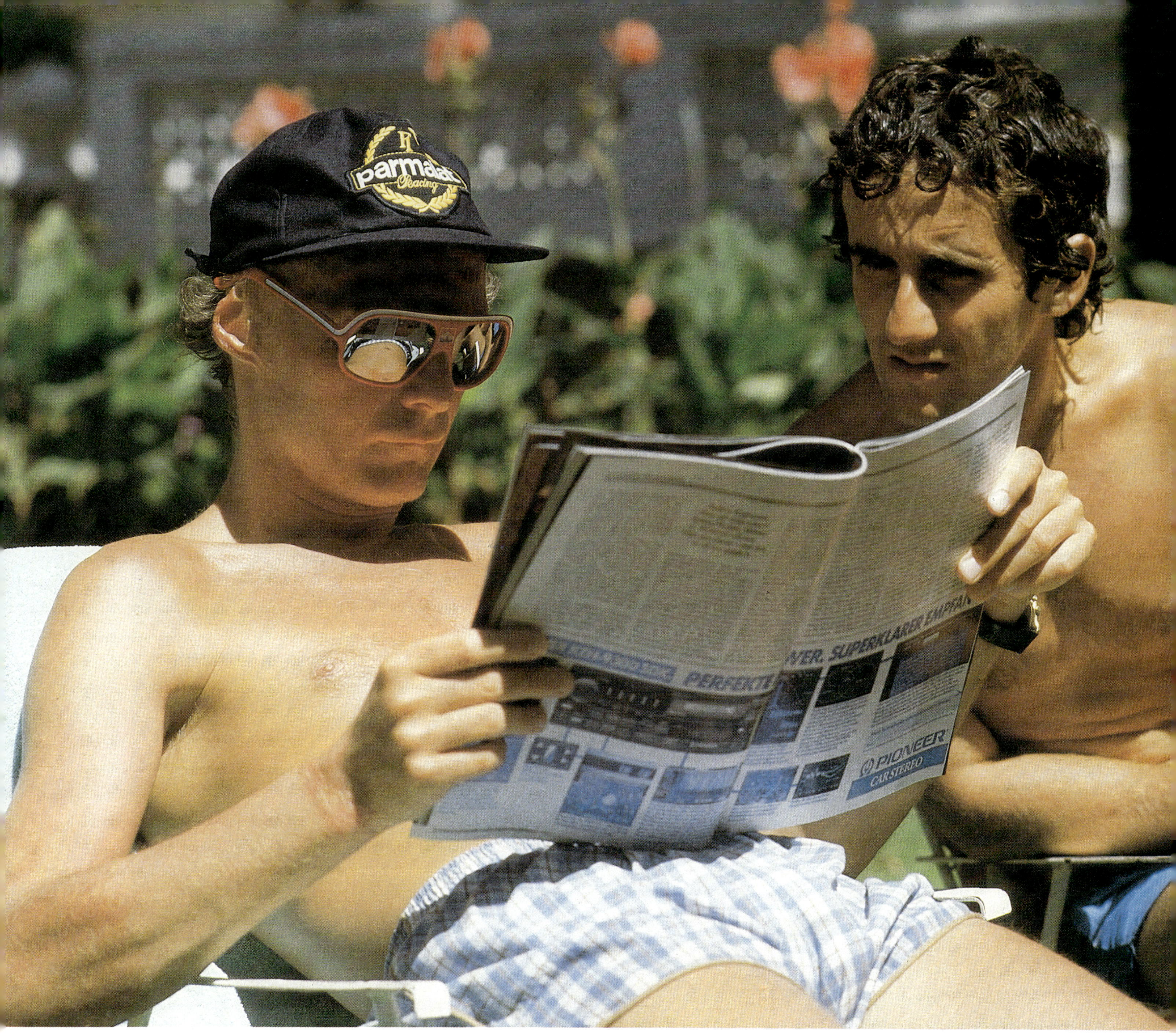
PERFEKTE
PIONEER
CAR STEREO

GILLES VILLENEUVE

Few Formula One drivers have had such an immediate impact on the sport or generated such enthusiasm and sheer adoration as Gilles Villeneuve, a French-Canadian who, during the four years he drove for Ferrari, constantly amazed his fellow-drivers with the acute angles his car achieved and the amount of time he would spend partly off the road. A fatal accident in practice brought his remarkable career to an abrupt end.

I find it hard to assess Villeneuve's calibre from the bare statistics of his brief, five-year career in Formula One. He scored just six wins in his 67 Grand Prix races. He was obviously quick, even wild. Who knows how he might have developed, given time? After his death, Enzo Ferrari commented, 'Villeneuve's personality captured the hearts of the crowds. He was the champion warrior and he gave Ferrari a great deal of fame. I was extremely fond of him.' It is sad, but true, that Ferrari would not often speak of his drivers with such affection until they were dead.

Villeneuve had his first racing experiences not on wheels but on ice. In his native Canada, he was a snow-mobile champion, skilled in travelling at high speeds in appalling conditions. This taught him the balance and control that were to be the hallmark of his driving.

After a string of successes in Formula Atlantic races in Canada, he was invited to drive a McLaren in the 1977 British Grand Prix at Silverstone. He spun the car several times. Some dismissed him as a crazy hot-head. Others were impressed, however, and, before the end of the season, he had been signed by Ferrari.

Above top: 1979, US Grand Prix East, Watkins Glen. Piano, piano... Tomaini seems to implore Gilles to take it easy. His pit signal tells him he is leading by 1 minute 35 seconds!
Above: 1981, Spanish Grand Prix, Jarama. Royal applause for Gilles from the King and Queen of Spain after his victory for Ferrari.

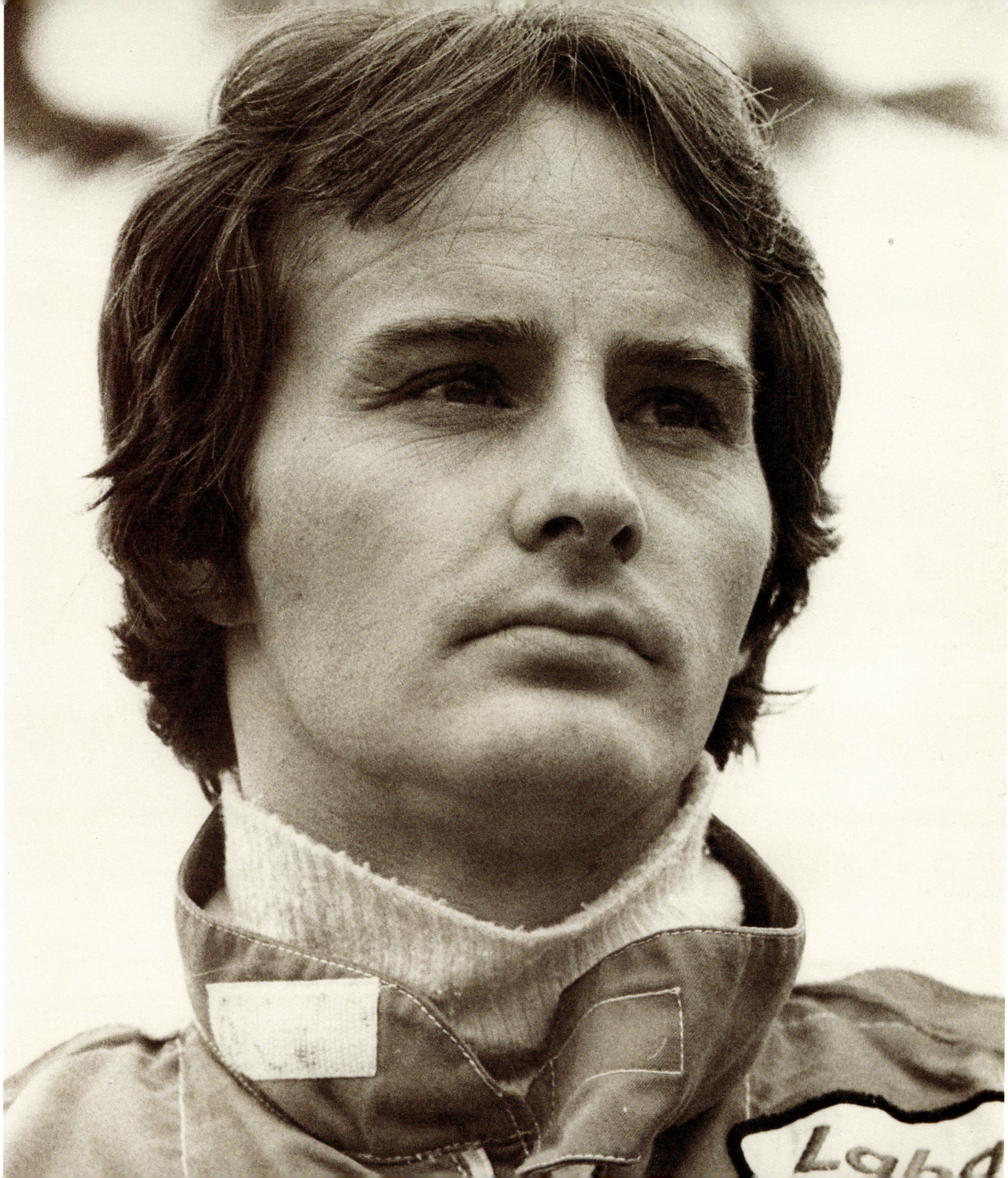

Gilles Villeneuve
FIAT
LONGINES
27
Agip
SMEG
MAGNETI MARELLI
personal
SCHMITTHELM
CHAMPION

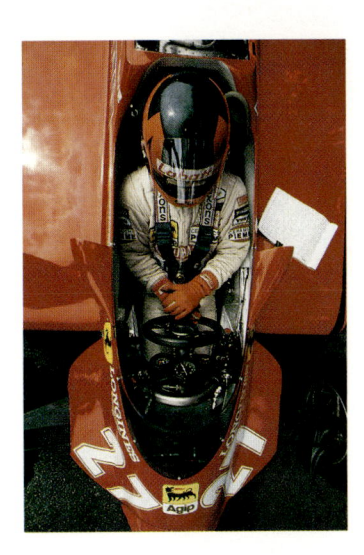

Villeneuve in the Ferrari No. 27, the number he made his own.

1982, Belgian Grand Prix, Zolder. Just before the crash that killed him, Gilles in No. 27, in practice for the race he never drove.

Left: 1981, Monaco Grand Prix. Ferrari No. 27 beats them all.

In the early eighties, the Ferrari rosse failed to match the power and efficiency of the opposition. But Villeneuve never gave up, often pushing his car beyond its capability, always demonstrating what Mauro Forghieri called 'a rage to win'.

Things looked more promising for Ferrari at the beginning of the 1982 season and success seemed within the grasp of Villeneuve and his team-mate, Pironi.

At Imola, in front of a vast crowd of cheering, flag-waving fans, Villeneuve, closely followed by Pironi, lay well clear of the field for the last twenty laps—a Ferrari 1-2 in Italy! In any team other than Ferrari they would have been told to hold position, but Pironi passed Villeneuve who shortly afterwards retook the lead only to have Pironi suddenly pull out of his slipstream half-way round the final lap to win.

Villeneuve was so incensed that, in a moment of anger, he vowed he'd never again speak to Pironi. Thirteen days later, during practice for the Belgian Grand Prix, Villeneuve set off determined to better Pironi's time.

Half-way round the circuit, approaching a fast right-hand curve, he clipped another car. His Ferrari flew into the air, catapulting him out of the cockpit and into the catch fencing. He died in hospital without recovering consciousness.

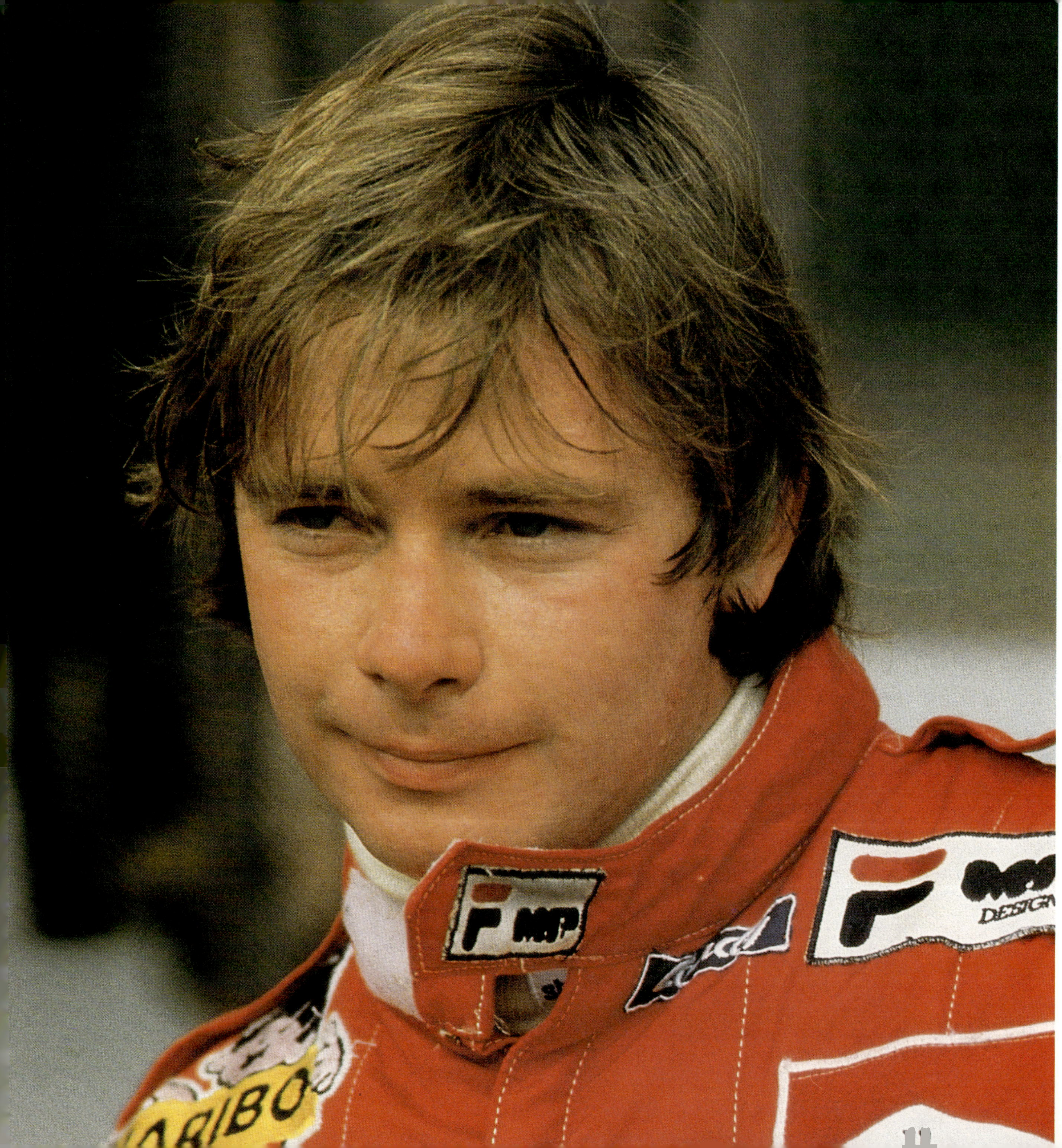

DIDIER PIRONI

A young, intelligent and very attractive Frenchman, Didier Pironi seemed to love to take risks for their own sake. By 1982, when his Grand Prix career was cut short by an appalling accident, he was fast becoming a calculating and complete driver.

In my view the fuel company Elf did more than any other body to bring France back to the sharp end of motor racing. During the late seventies and early eighties it offered consistent support to French teams and sponsored its own driver development programme. From this sprang Alain Prost; so also did Didier Pironi.

The 1978 season was the first for Pironi, who, as I myself had done in my first year, drove for Ken Tyrrell. He instantly made a strong impression as a competitor. In those early days he wasn't over-competitive against two other Frenchmen, Patrick Depailler and Jean-Pierre Jarier, but when he joined Jacques Laffite at Ligier he began to show his true speed. By beating his team-leader on seven occasions in 1980 and winning at Zolder, Pironi attracted the attention of Enzo Ferrari, who must have thought: This young Frenchman is just the kind of man to put alongside Gilles Villeneuve—each will inspire the other.

Recognizing that Pironi was a real fighter who had 'fire in his belly', Ferrari recruited the young Frenchman for the 1981 season. Later he recalled, 'As soon as Pironi arrived at Maranello, he won everyone's admiration and affection, not only for his gifts as an athlete, but also for his way of doing things—he was reserved while at the same time outgoing.'

It was not to be easy for Didier, for he soon fell

Above top: 1980, Belgian Grand Prix, Zolder. Pironi was the victor for Ligier-Ford and team-mate Jacques Laffite put up the fastest lap.
Above: Pironi ready to race.
Left: Pironi and his bride on their wedding day.

131

1980, Belgian Grand Prix, Zolder. Pironi on his way to victory.

1982, Monaco. Pironi in the Ferrari No. 28.

John Surtees remembers, 'After his accident in practice at Hockenheim in 1982, I went to see Pironi in hospital. He told me that he was persistently challenging medical opinion in the hope that he would race again, and that Enzo Ferrari kept in constant touch on the telephone, with the promise of an automatic gearbox being fitted to his car on his return.'

Team-mates confer—Pironi and Laffite.

Far right: 1987, St Tropez. A competitor to his fingertips, Didier Pironi racing an offshore powerboat—the sport in which he was to die later that same year.

foul of Ferrari's habit of setting his drivers against each other, and Villeneuve—a flamboyant, somewhat reckless number one—was already well entrenched at Maranello. I believe that Pironi decided to bide his time and work patiently to overcome the stigma of being number two to Villeneuve. Clearly he had hopes that 1982 would be his year. At San Marino, he forced his way past the unsuspecting Villeneuve during the last lap and snatched first place. Still the dispute goes on: What exactly were the team orders, and what did the pit signals mean? They may have meant 'Hold position'. Did Didier put one over on Villeneuve?

During practice for the next Grand Prix at Zolder, Villeneuve crashed to his death. Pironi went on to score a first, two seconds and two thirds in five out of the next six races. Then came the German GP at Hockenheim.

As number one at Ferrari, he may have felt that to succeed he must seize every opportunity to shine—that I can well understand. Yet he had already won pole position when he set off again in the rain on an untimed practice run. Blinded by spray, he struck Alain Prost's Renault. His Ferrari was seen to shoot high into the air, land tail first and cartwheel to the side of the track. Miraculously, Pironi, his right foot smashed, was still alive.

For many agonising months, Pironi put up a desperate but unsuccessful fight to regain his fitness and return to motor racing. Somehow, he had to satisfy the competitive urge that still drove him, so he turned instead to powerboat racing. Ironically, he was killed in an accident off the Isle of Wight in August 1987.

DIDIER PIRONI

ALAIN PROST

Known as 'The Professor', Alain Prost is one of the most complete drivers of all time. Like his idol, Jim Clark, he has a fluid, natural driving style which makes difficult manoeuvres look simple. Three times world champion, he has won more Formula One Grands Prix than any other driver.

1985, Austrian Grand Prix. Prost not only took first place but set the fastest lap for McLaren-TAG.

Far right: Prost always keeps cool, especially here on the occasion of the Prix Afrique du Sud.

To become the world champion, a driver has to be single-minded, consistent and skilled, but, above all else, he must be in the right car. That is more than ever important in today's high-tech world of computerized engines and special mix high-octane fuel. When, as has so often happened in recent years, one constructor has a car or engine that is noticeably superior to all others, the would-be champion is likely to find his closest competitor is the other member of his team.

Despite what journalists have said, I have never

1981, French Grand Prix, Dijon. Prost's first Grand Prix victory was, fittingly, in a Renault on his home ground. The start of a stunningly successful career.

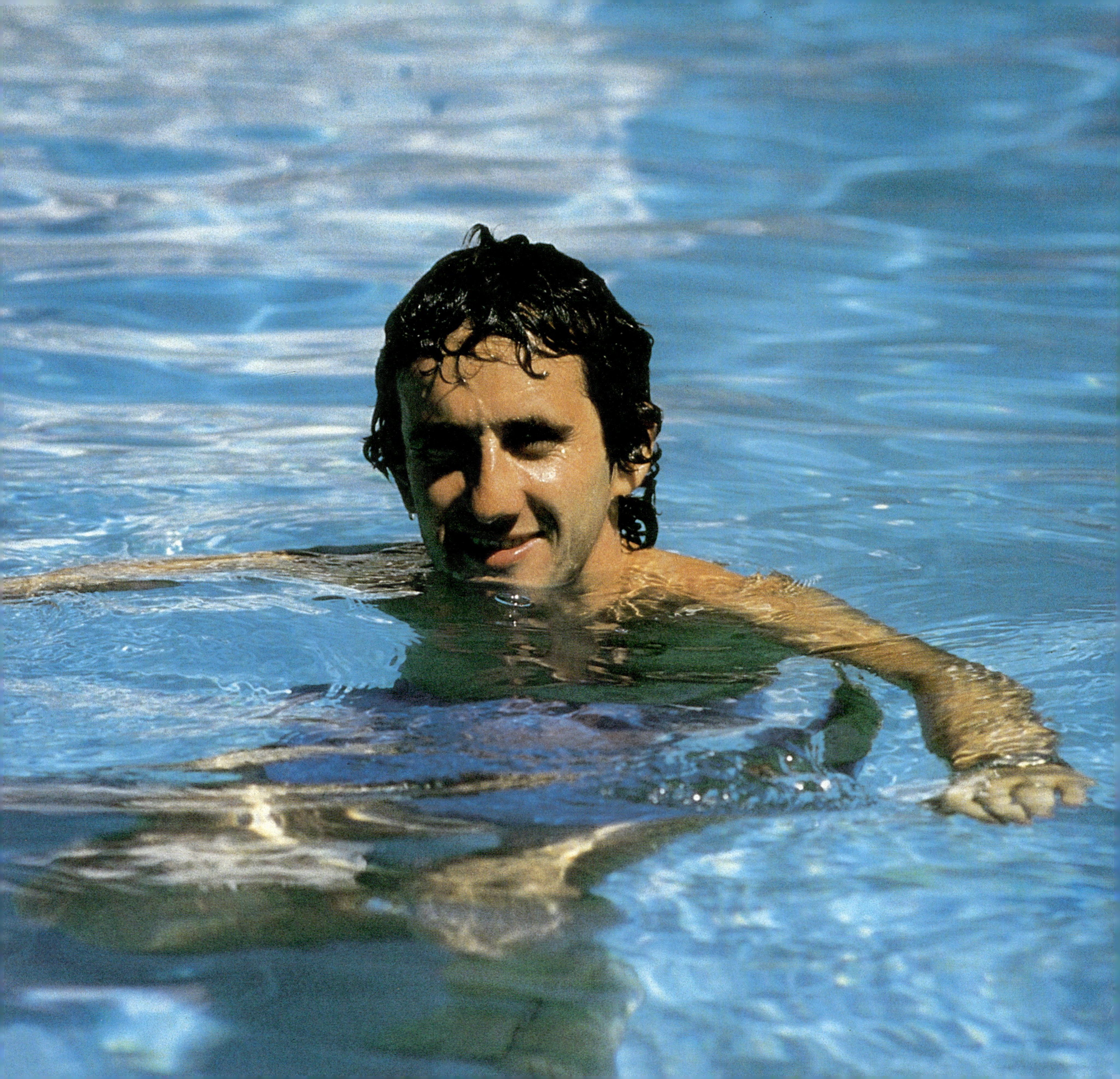

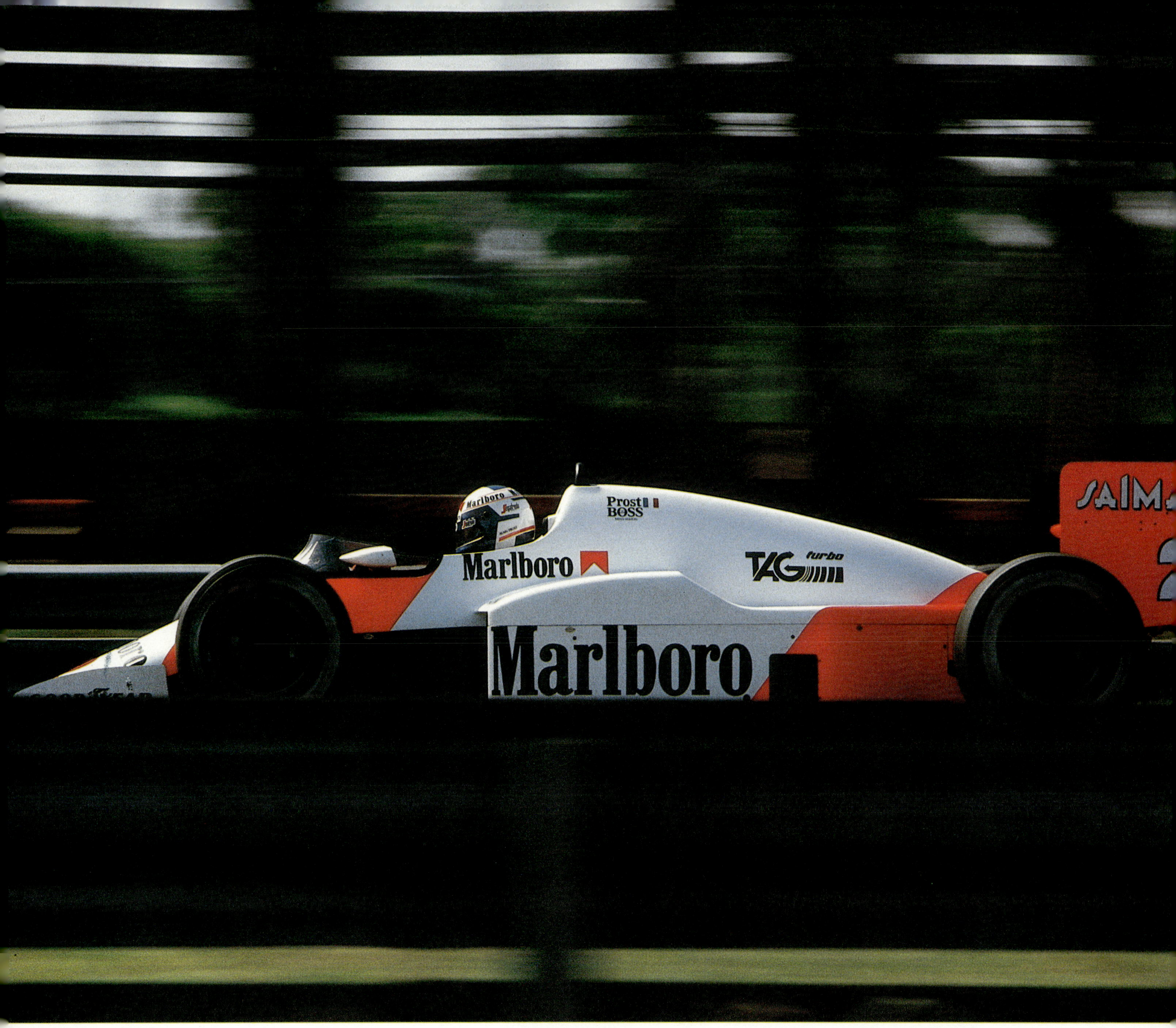
Marlboro
Prost
BOSS
Marlboro
TAG turbo
Marlboro

ALAIN PROST

Left: 1985, Brazilian Grand Prix. Prost won this first Grand Prix of the season, his McLaren-TAG beating Michele Alboreto in a Ferrari by more than 3 seconds.

Enjoying his push-ups! Prost keeps himself in trim.

driven for a team where I was ordered to be number one or number two. To be designated number one, that driver must be seen to be the best. For much of his career, Prost has faced that challenge.

With the ever increasing attention paid by the media to Formula One racing, much has been made of what drivers have said in public. This unfortunate trend has perhaps distracted many of us from the unquestionable driving skills of my last three racing heroes—Prost, Mansell and Senna, but I have selected them for their achievements on the track—not for what they may have said or done off it—and I cannot but wish that many of their utterances had been made in private.

Prost began racing as a teenager in France—first in go-carts and then in Formula Renault. In 1978, he switched to Formula Three, winning the European championship the following year. In 1980, aged 24, he joined the McLaren Formula One team. It was not a happy year for Prost. The car was plagued with problems and, at the end of the season, he signed for Renault as the number two driver to René Arnoux.

From the start, Prost was the faster of the two.

ALAIN PROST

He won three Grands Prix and finished well ahead of Arnoux in the drivers' championship. During the next season, the rivalry between the two men intensified and their relationship deteriorated—a fact much commented upon in the French press. The 1982 season was only moderately successful for Renault and, at the end of it, Arnoux left to join Ferrari.

With only the South African Grand Prix to come in the 1983 season, Prost was leading the title race by two points from Nelson Piquet. After 36 laps, he was forced to retire. He watched from the pits as Piquet finished third and snatched the world championship by two points.

In some sections of the French press, Prost was accused of having wilfully thrown away the title. Renault sacked him and, within days, he'd signed again for McLaren. This time his team-mate was Niki Lauda, who had returned to Formula One racing determined to prove he could again win the world championship. In 1984 he did—by half a point from Prost.

The positions were reversed in 1985, when Prost romped home with the title in what was to be Lauda's last year in Formula One. Prost retained the world championship in 1986 but, at the beginning of the next season, he was joined at McLaren by Senna, the aggressive and committed Brazilian driver. A new and even more intense rivalry had begun.

Fighting against the supremacy of the Williams-Honda team, neither Prost nor Senna was close to winning the 1987 championship, but in 1988 the Honda engine went to McLaren and the battle of the season was between only two men. Of the 16 Grands Prix, seven

1989. Alain Prost turns to current affairs.

1990, Canadian Grand Prix. Prost sidelined in practice.

Far right: 1988, San Marino Grand Prix. An unlikely couple—Prost hams it for the photographers with one of Honda's hot machines, while Senna forces a grin.

138

139

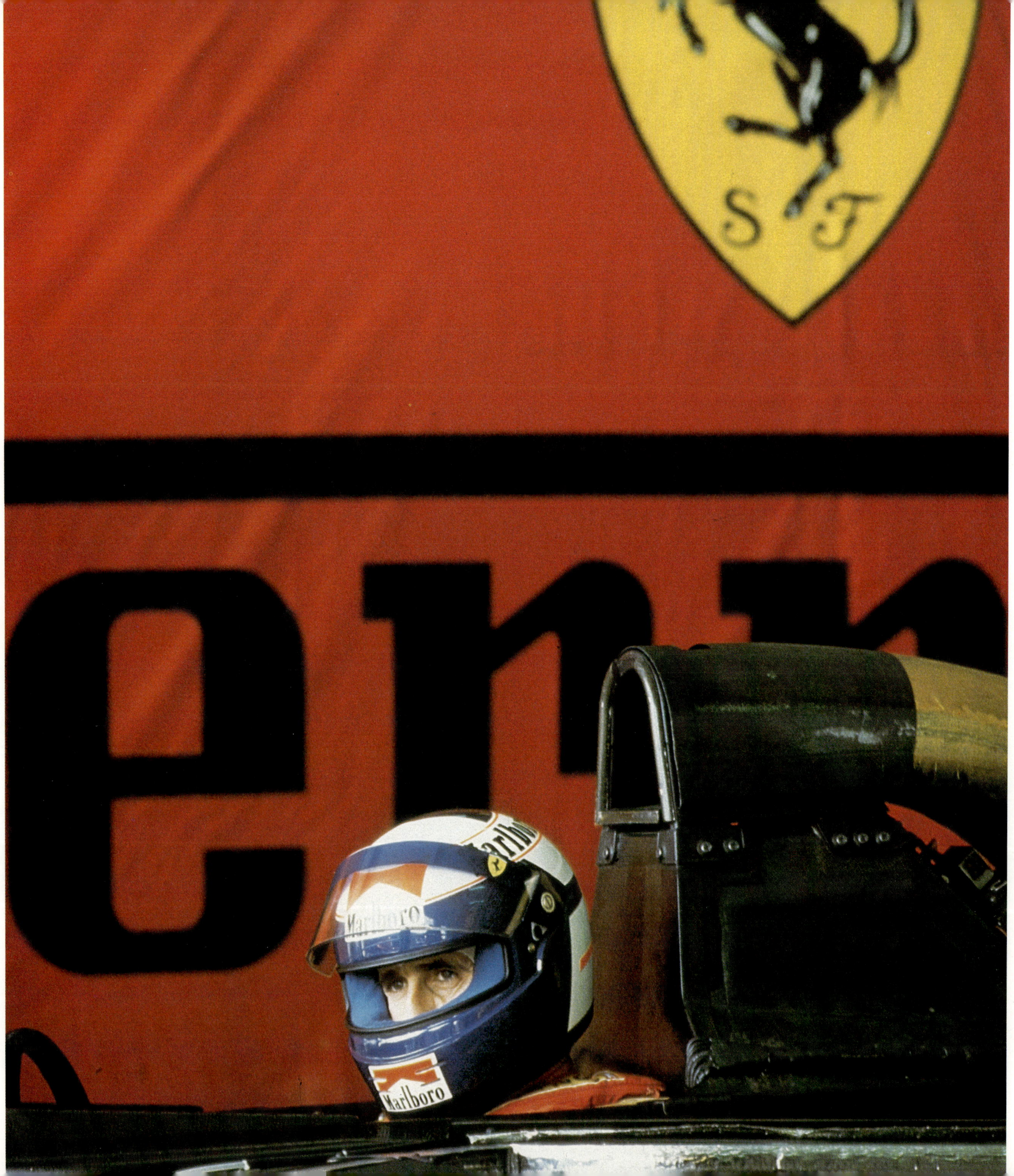
Marlboro
Marlboro

went to Prost and eight to Senna, who won the world championship from his team-mate by only three points.

The bitter and at times controversial duel between the two McLaren drivers also dominated the 1989 season. At Imola, Senna broke what Prost has said was a pre-race agreement not to overtake before the first corner. Half-way through the same season, Prost made public his suspicions that his own engine was not being as well-prepared as Senna's. This statement brought no credit to Prost, and only served to emphasise the pressure he was being put under by Senna. But in Japan he seized the lead and held it for 43 laps. Not until the closing stages could Senna mount the challenge which brought them together. Both cars slithered to a halt and Prost retired. Senna recovered and went on to win, only to be disqualified, in my view wrongly. So Prost, with one round to go, was already world champion for the third time.

Prost left McLaren at the end of 1989 to join Mansell at Ferrari. The honeymoon period between the two was soon over as Prost outmanoeuvred and outraced his established team-mate. In July 1990, after Prost had won four Grands Prix, Mansell, who had won none at that stage, stepped down.

The battle for the 1990 championship was again between Prost and Senna. By the Japanese Grand Prix, Senna was certain of the title if Prost won no further points. Prost, in my opinion, made a serious error of judgement in the way he set up his car for the first corner, an error he could not afford with Senna alongside him and a championship at stake. Again the cars came together, and Prost's hopes of winning his forty-fifth Grand Prix and his fourth world championship vanished for the season.

1990. Prost faces the press.

Left: 1991. Prost reflects upon turbulent times at Ferrari.

Above top: 1991, Australian Grand Prix. The split. This newspaper placard shouts the news of the parting of the ways between Alain Prost and Scuderia Ferrari. Above: 1991, Belgian Grand Prix. Times are tough for Alain Prost.

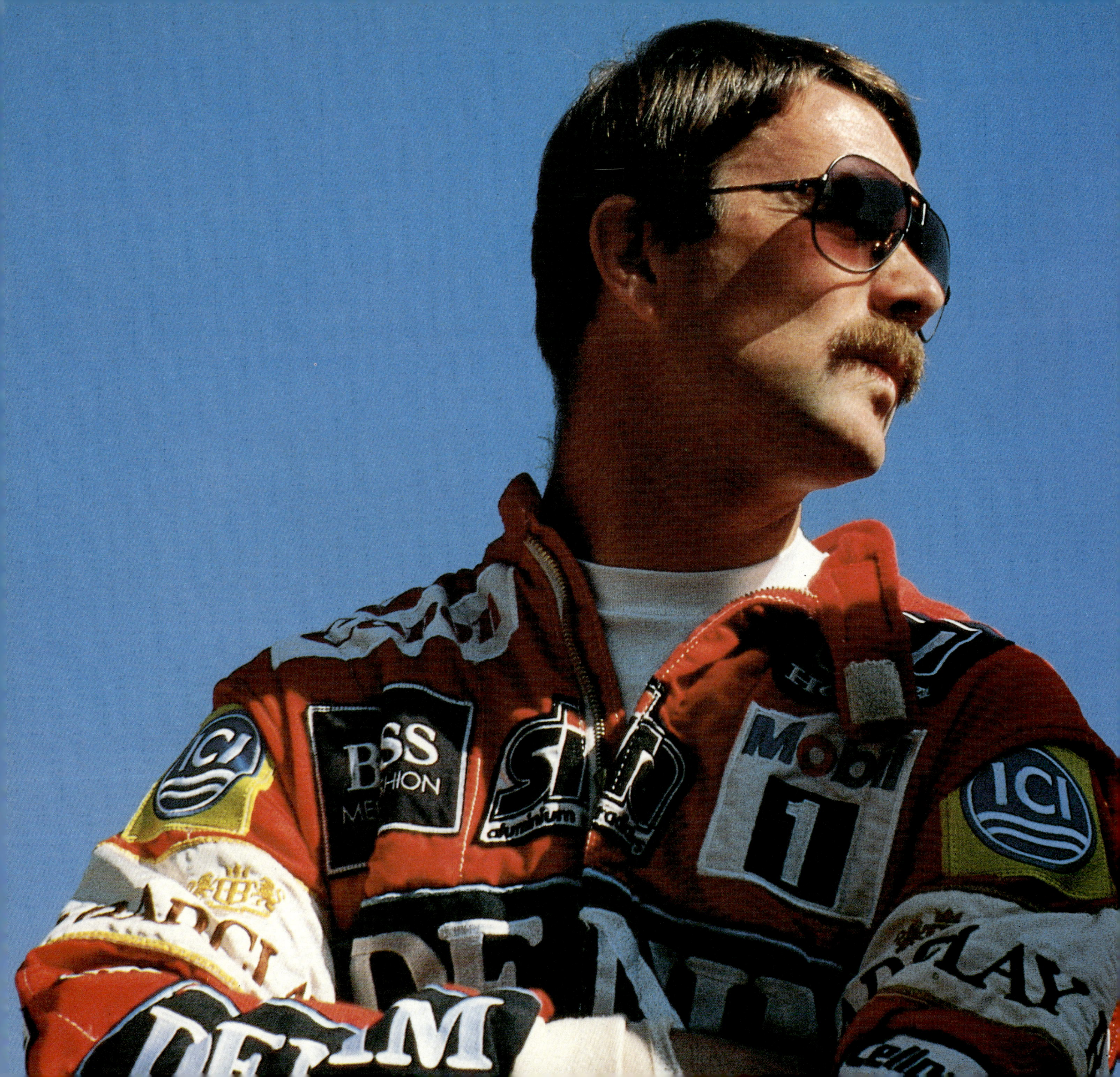
ICI
Mobil
1
ICI

PIRELLI ALBUM OF MOTOR RACING HEROES

NIGEL MANSELL

For the best part of a decade, British hopes have rested on Nigel Mansell to become Britain's first world champion since James Hunt in 1976. As we go to press, 1992 has seen him score a record five Formula One firsts in succession and win the world championship in the single-minded style that he has made his own.

1981, Canadian Grand Prix. Boss Colin Chapman has a quiet word with Mansell.

1986, French Grand Prix. What was to become a regular performance by Nigel Mansell—victory and the fastest lap, this time for Williams-Honda.

There can be little doubt that Nigel Mansell has the determination and the will to win. He progressed through Formula Ford and Formula Three, having his fair share of accidents, but was fortunate to have the wholehearted support of his wife Rosanne. She even agreed to the sale of their house and car so that he could stay in the sport. I should add that Nigel is only one of many aspiring racers who have done this.

In 1979 Colin Chapman, always on the lookout for talent, suggested a test drive in a Lotus Formula One at Paul Ricard, that superb facility in the South of France. Although a drive in the March Formula Three had involved him in a crash with Andrea de Cesaris only two days earlier, Nigel drove with enough confidence and precision to be given a testing contract by Colin, which brought with it the chance regularly to drive a Formula One car. A contract of this kind also tied drivers of racing potential to Chapman.

Later that year he got his chance in Austria where he qualified on the back row of the grid. He afterwards recalled that from the start fuel was leaking into the cockpit and soaking into his overalls and thermal underwear—a 'hot seat' of an extremely uncomfortable sort, as I know from personal experience. Mansell lasted 41 laps before engine failure brought his ordeal to an end.

It wasn't until 1981 that Mansell's perseverance paid off and he became a full-time member of Team Lotus, an arrangement which was to continue for the

Right: 1986, British Grand Prix. Nigel chats to his friend, pop singer Leo Sayer.

Right: 1987, Austrian Grand Prix. Strain and emotion course through Nigel Mansell after his victory.

Far right: 1987, San Marino Grand Prix. Nigel streaks to victory in the Williams-Honda.

Golf enthusiast Mansell in the 1991 Nick Faldo Challenge at Quietwaters, British Columbia.

next four years, though he could never be sure from year to year whether his contract would be renewed. But he clearly showed ability or Chapman would not have kept him on, and he was placed several times.

In 1985, Frank Williams, as had Chapman before him, spotted Mansell's potential and signed him as a backup to Keke Rosberg. Constructors need results, and perhaps they came a little earlier than expected for Frank. Nigel scored two consecutive victories—the European Grand Prix at Silverstone followed by the South African GP at Kyalami, a win which he repeated on the re-styled Kyalami circuit in 1992.

At the end of 1985, Nigel's new team-mate was to be Nelson Piquet and they were to drive the new Honda-powered Williams. In 1986 Piquet won the first race in Brazil, Mansell having clashed with Senna. The next Grand Prix, in Spain, gave us the sort of racing we all like to see. Mansell, after changing tyres, put on an incredible charge to catch Alain Prost and Ayrton Senna, who had about 20 seconds advantage. He overtook Prost and, at the chequered flag, was virtually level with Senna who won by a mere 0.01 of a second.

Mansell went on that year to win five races in the Williams-Honda, including the British Grand Prix at Brands Hatch. Afterwards, Tadashi Kume, the Honda president who had been partly responsible for engine design and development when I'd driven for Honda during their early incursions into Formula One in 1967 and 1968, sent me a telegram which read, 'Without your contribution, none of this would have been possible.'

NIGEL MANSELL

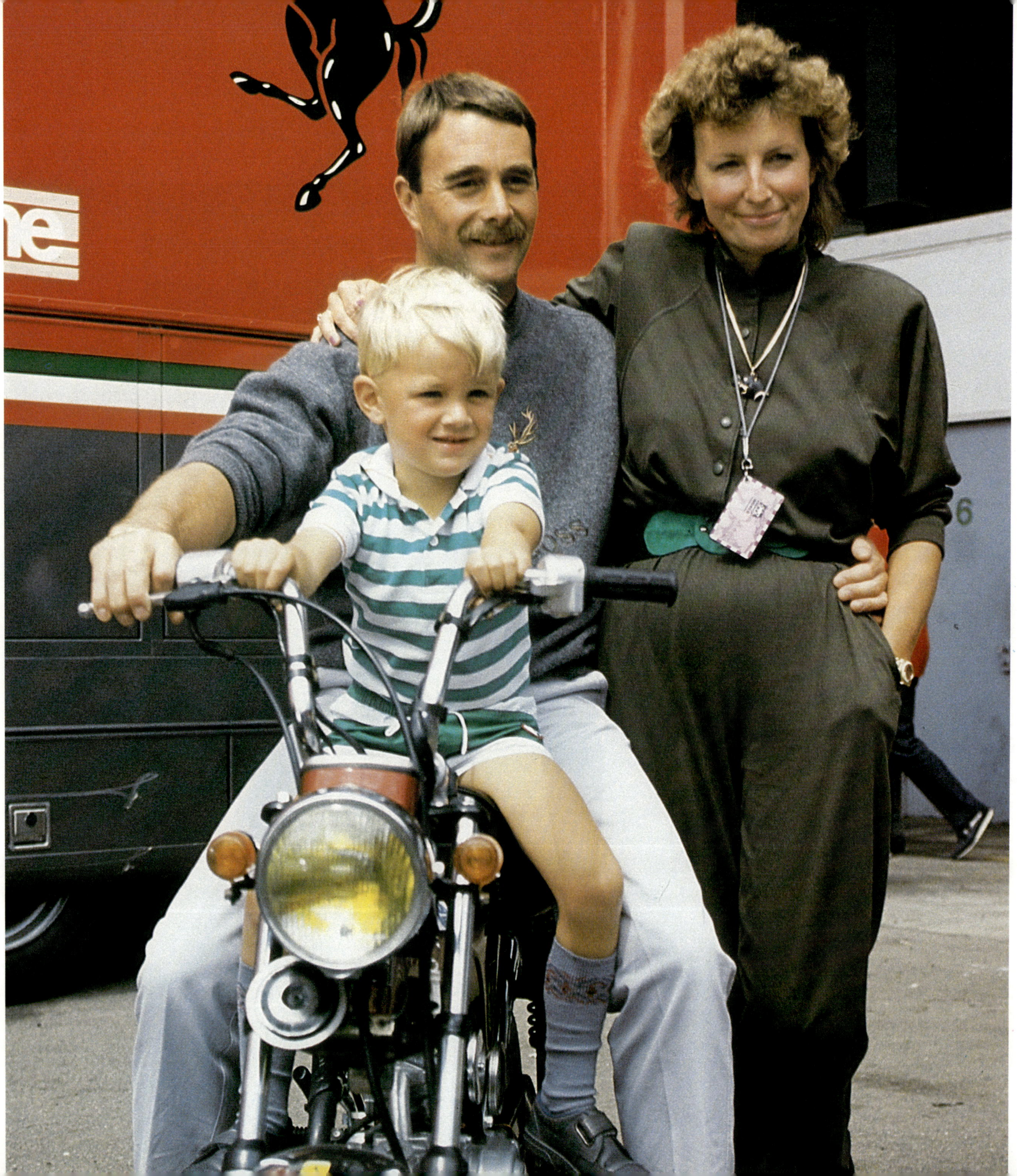

Left: 1989, British Grand Prix. Nigel, Rosanne and Leo Mansell in the paddock.

1989, Brazilian Grand Prix. Nigel after his truly lion-hearted drive, the first time he drove for real for Ferrari.

1989, Brazilian Grand Prix. So tired he can hardly raise the trophy in triumph, Nigel after his win in the new Ferrari 640.

Despite scoring more victories than any other driver, Mansell lost the 1986 Formula One World Championship to Prost by two points. There was an almost identical result in 1987. Mansell won six Grands Prix, while Piquet, his team-mate, won only three but captured the title because of his better finishing record.

In the 1988 season, it was no surprise that McLaren and not Williams had secured the Honda engine, for Mansell had not endeared himself to Honda by complaining that the engines he had been given were second-best. I met Nigel in Adelaide at the end of the season, after it had been announced that he was to join Ferrari. I asked him whether he would be testing the new Ferrari at the imminent session, and he replied that his contract would be for a year, and that if Ferrari wanted him to test before his work was due to start then they must give him another contract. This answer in my opinion sums up why he failed at Ferrari and Prost was able to take the initiative. But in the very first race of the season, the Brazilian Grand Prix, driving the new Ferrari 640 he dominated the race and won. However, there was to be only one other victory for Mansell in the 1989 season. In 1990 he was joined at Ferrari by Prost, who, with his more fluent Italian, enjoyed a honeymoon period which undermined Mansell's contribution to the team. As Prost won races and he did not,

1991, British Grand Prix, Silverstone. They've had their differences, but what can you do when a colleague needs a lift after the race? Mansell did just that—on his way to the pits with Ayrton Senna.

1991, British Grand Prix, Silverstone. Crusaders for the Lionheart—Nigel's fans ecstatic at his home victory.

1992, South African Grand Prix, Kyalami. A 1-2 for the Williams-Renault pair—Mansell and Riccardo Patrese at the new circuit. Michael Schumacher, a superstar in the making, drove brilliantly to third place for Benetton-Ford.

Far right: 1990 season. Nigel in what would seem to be dejected conversation with boss-of-the-moment at Ferrari, Cesare Fiorio.

Mansell began to despair and, in July, he announced his retirement from Formula One racing.

I was not altogether surprised when, three months later, he changed his mind. Clearly the racer in Mansell had won the argument. His expectations for the new season to win the championship were almost fulfilled. However, a human error, under pressure, in the normally super-efficient Williams team led to an illegal push start and Mansell's disqualification from the Portuguese Grand Prix—which he was leading—and a loss of valuable championship points.

Yet again, Japan was to be the scene of the championship decider. While attacking Senna in the McLaren-Honda, Nigel, in a Williams-Renault, went off the road. Senna became world champion for a third time and Mansell a worthy but frustrated runner-up.

There was little by way of frustration in 1992. The Hungarian Grand Prix clinched that elusive world championship for Mansell, in his sensationally fast and reliable Williams–Renault, with five of the season's sixteen races still to go. Much has been said in the press about Mansell's tendency to complain, and I have often felt that he could be his own worst enemy. He has had both good and bad luck and has driven some brilliant and aggressive races. I just hope that he can now let his performances on the track speak for themselves.

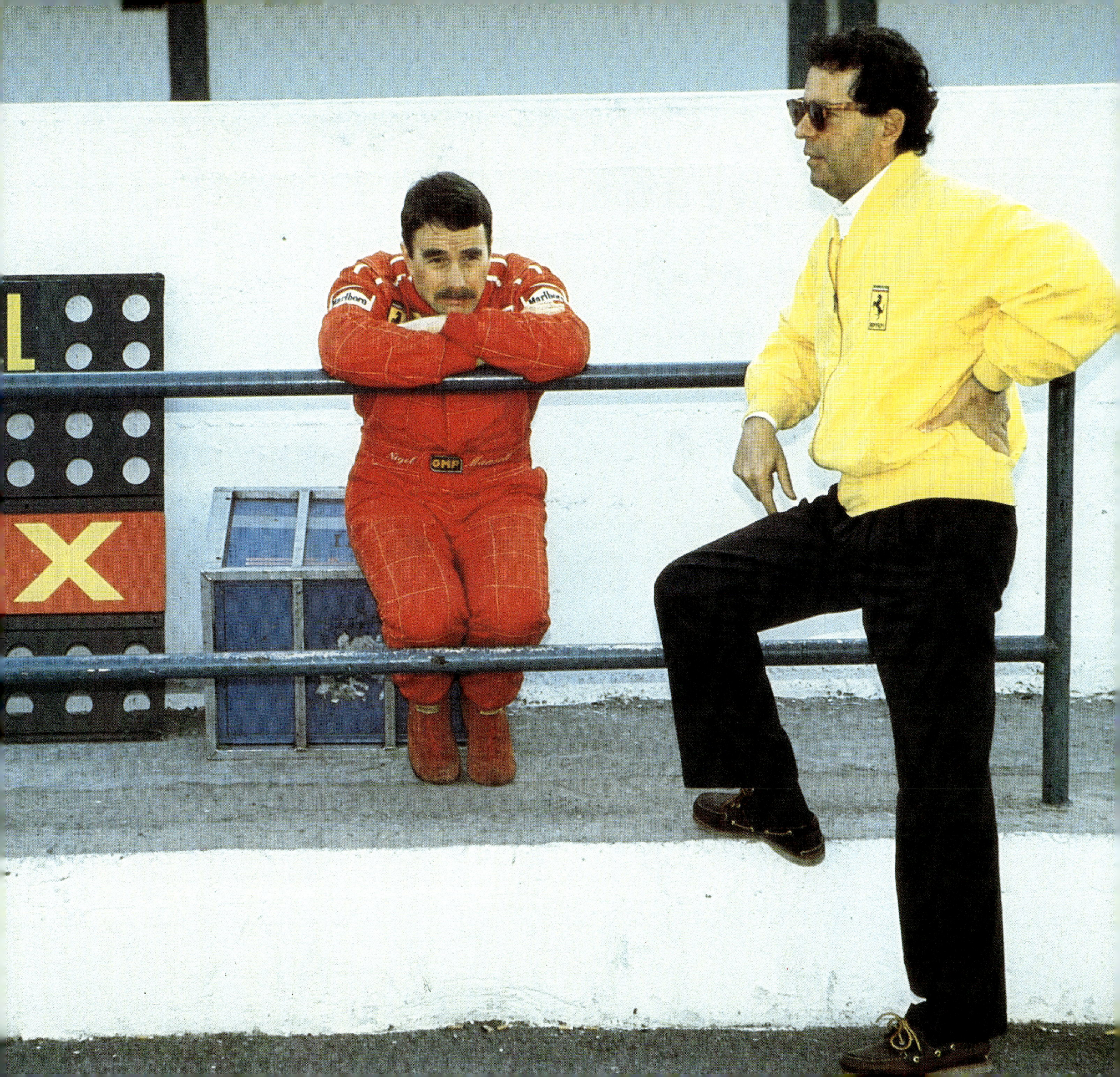
L
X
Marlboro
Marlboro
OMP

AYRTON SENNA

There have been few more dedicated, determined and successful competitors in motor racing than Brazil's triple world champion, Ayrton Senna. At the start of his career he said, 'There is no room in my life for anything but motor racing.' That statement would still seem to be true.

Above right: 1984, Monaco Grand Prix. Torrential rain stopped the race after only 31 of its 77 laps, by which time Senna had worked his way up to second place in his Toleman-Hart.

Right: 1984. Ayrton Senna deep in thought as he checks practice lap times.

Formula One racing has always been largely the domain of European constructors and drivers. There has usually been an Australasian and American presence. In recent years, Japanese engineering genius and finance have had a decisive impact on results and brought to the Grand Prix circuits a few Japanese drivers. But Brazil is the country outside Europe which has produced the most world champions.

The first Brazilian to win the title was Fittipaldi—in 1972 and 1974. His fellow-countryman, Nelson Piquet, won it three times—in 1981, 1983 and 1987. The most recent and brilliant of the Brazilian champions is Ayrton Senna, winner in 1988, 1990 and 1991.

I drove against Senna once. It was at an event organized by Mercedes-Benz in 1984 to launch their 190 saloon. Some ex-world champions and a few new-comers were invited to race the cars round the new Nürburgring. While most drivers in practice were running over the grass in their efforts to straighten the corners, I noticed that Senna, then only 24, drove with that absolute precision which we have all now been privileged to see. He kept all four wheels on the track, just clipping the kerbs and verges. He won the race.

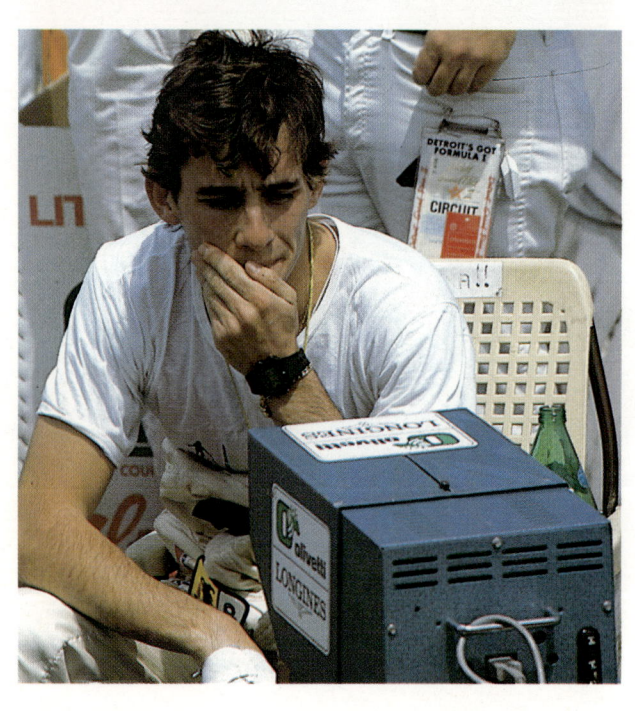

I was impressed. A little later, I dropped a note to Ferrari saying, 'Senna is a man to have on your team.'

150

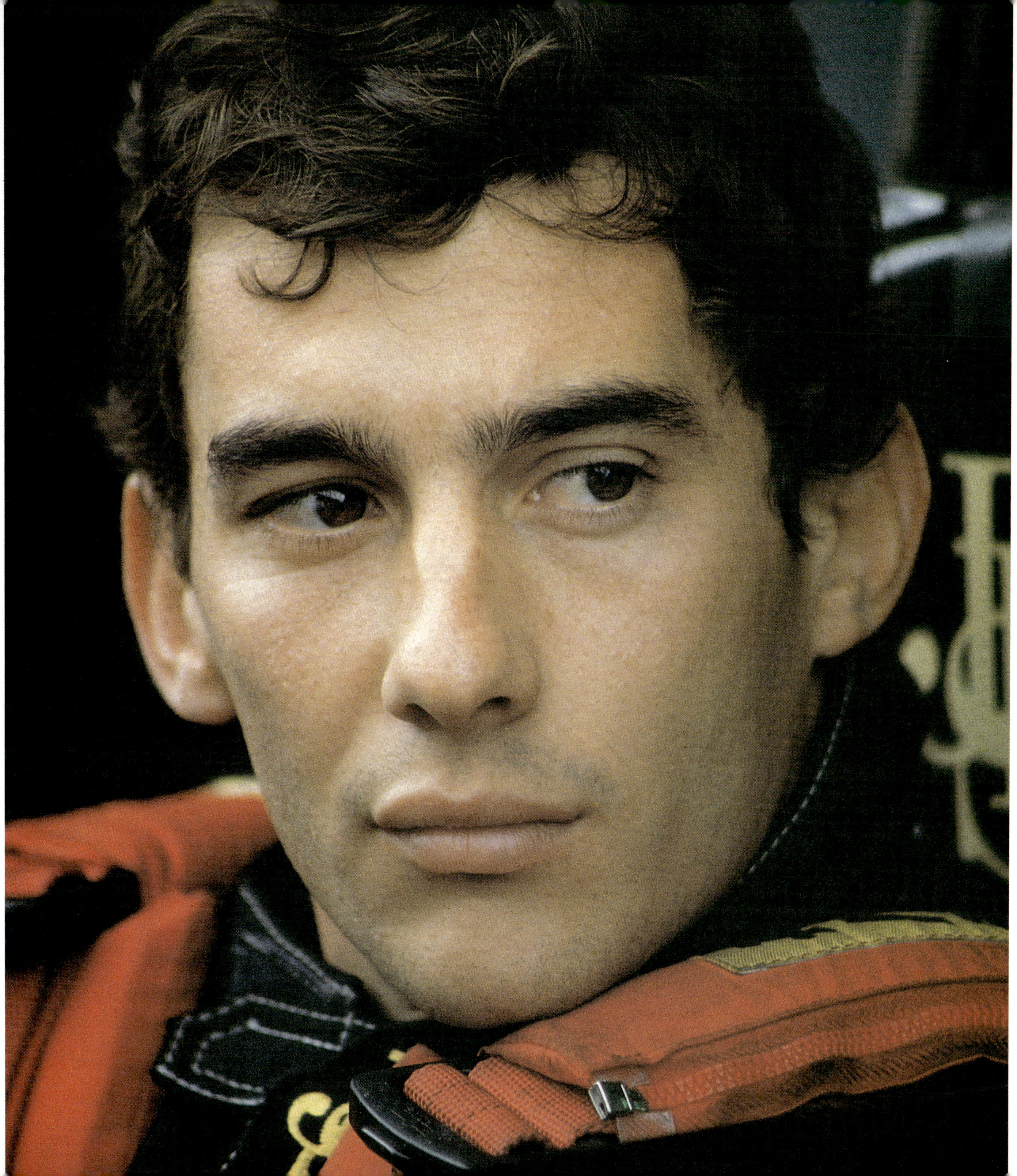

John Player Special
John Player
RENAULT
elf
John Player Special
John Player Special
OLYMPUS
CAMERAS
12
elf
RENAULT
GOODYEAR
GOODYEAR

Left: 1985, Portuguese Grand Prix. After Ayrton Senna's astonishing victory for Lotus-Renault in heavy rain, everyone knew he was destined for stardom, but perhaps could not at the time envisage the megastar status he was to achieve.

Red, white, and winning—this is how we have been used to seeing Ayrton Senna.

1988, Australian Grand Prix, Adelaide. A moment of mutual respect. Senna holds Prost's arm aloft in public salute after coming second to Alain in a 1-2 for McLaren-Honda.

At the time, Senna was in his first Formula One season, driving for the Toleman team. The previous year, he'd been the British Formula Three champion, winning a record nine races in succession. He was less successful with Toleman but, despite his car's limitations, he came second in the rain-shortened Monaco Grand Prix. In the 1984 world championship, he finished equal ninth with Nigel Mansell.

At the end of the season, Senna bought himself out of his three-year contract with Toleman and signed for Lotus. In 1985, he drove with smooth precision through a rainstorm to win the Portuguese Grand Prix. During that season, he held pole position seven times and came fourth in the drivers' championship. The following year, he again finished fourth with two Grand Prix wins. In 1987, he was third.

He then joined Alain Prost in the McLaren team which, having obtained the Honda engine, was due once again to dominate Grand Prix racing. In the 16 races of 1988, McLaren won all but one—eight went to Senna and seven to Prost. Senna, who started in pole position 13 times, was the season's world champion.

The intense rivalry between the two McLaren

AYRTON SENNA

Getting away from it all—but only up to a point. Ayrton Senna indulging his hobby of flying model aeroplanes, Silverstone, 1988.

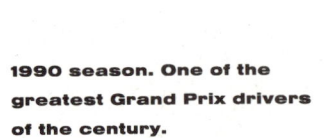

1990 season. One of the greatest Grand Prix drivers of the century.

Far right: 1991, French Grand Prix. Senna won the championship, but he did not win the race. Ayrton and the McLaren-Honda next to the matching kerb. He finished third.

drivers continued throughout 1989 and Senna just lost the title to Prost who then signed for Ferrari. The 1990 world championship was an equally close battle between the two bitter rivals, but Senna in his McLaren, with its Honda V10 engine, was the victor. In 1991, after a mighty tussle with Mansell, he won his third title with seven Grand Prix wins.

His racing record is outstanding. Not only has he won three world championships in four years, he has started from pole position more times than any other driver and up to the end of 1991 only Prost had achieved more Grand Prix victories.

I have often wondered why it is that, despite these successes, Senna isn't universally praised or admired. Some press reporters have suggested that he has upset almost all his fellow-drivers and many of the vast army of motor racing pundits. Frankly, I find such reports exaggerated. Controversial he has certainly been. When Senna has given post-race press conferences, he has at times seemed bored and distant, giving his answers in monosyllables. Here I believe he has been misunderstood. People forget that English is not his native language. Also, they may not realise that not all journalists really understand what today's motor racing is all about. It's hard to be a reporter of motor sport. Few have ever been directly involved or understood its technical complexities. Perhaps the press have simply found Senna too single-minded in his attitude to his chosen sport, even too successful, and Senna himself is reticent by nature.

154

Marlboro
Marlboro
HONDA
COURTAULDS
COURTAULDS
Shell
Shell
Marlboro
HONDA
1
TAG HEUER
Shell
Shell

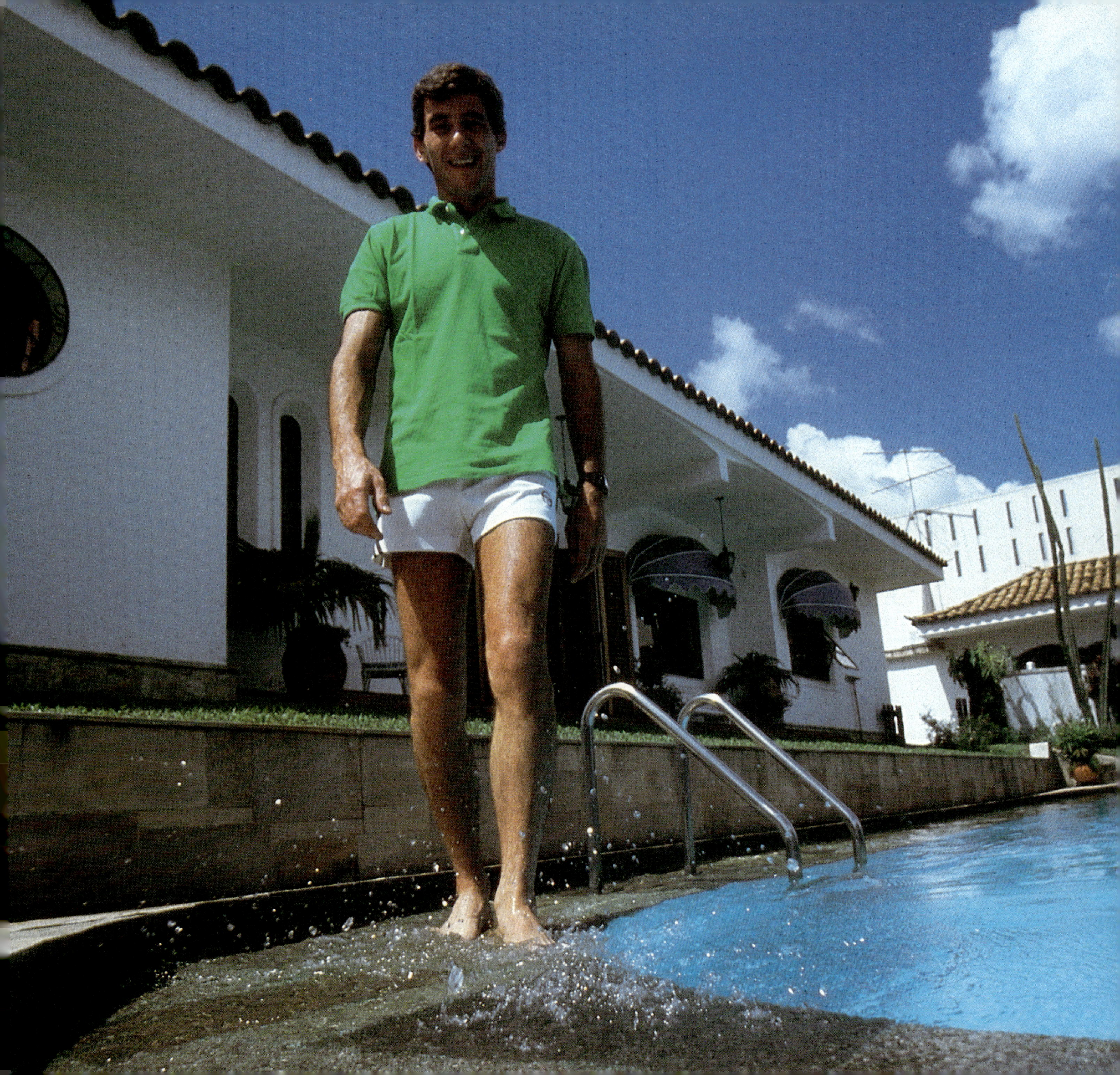

1991, Brazilian Grand Prix. A deafening roar as the vast crowd bellowed approval at Senna's home win in the McLaren-Honda.

1991, Hungarian Grand Prix. This is how it ended at the Hungaroring—Senna first in the McLaren-Honda and Nigel Mansell second in the Williams-Renault. That's how the championship ended, too.

Left: Ayrton at home relaxes by the pool.

But it is his tactics on the track that have created the greatest controversies, especially those involving his former team-mate Prost. At Portugal in 1988, as Prost pulled out of his slipstream Senna appeared to swerve to the right, almost pushing Prost into the wall. The incidents involving them in the Japanese Grands Prix of 1989 and 1990, were not, in my opinion, mistakes on the part of Senna. I believe that each one was compounded by grave errors of judgement on Prost's part, and by the sheer ability that he met at the hands of Senna.

Without doubt there is something obsessive—and, for spectators, breathtakingly exciting—about the precision and total commitment of Senna's driving. However, his considerable skills are much underrated in some quarters. On the racing circuits he is very much a loner, which makes him a man after my own heart. He spends endless hours testing his cars, talking to mechanics and rehearsing forthcoming races. He is an extremely religious man, who believes he has been privileged to see God and feel his power. Unlike some other successful drivers, he doesn't seem over-interested in the trappings of wealth. Senna is very much the outsider in the tightly-held world of Formula One, and this may make him the more formidable.

But he is also one of the most masterful of racing drivers, with an unshakeable resolve to be the best. He has said, 'The most important thing for me is to win. The few seconds of pleasure I get when I overtake, or gain a pole position, or win a race are my motivation.'

AN UNSUNG HERO

Grand Prix racing has always been a collaboration between manufacturers, a host of accessory and component suppliers, and an army of technical experts. Today's space-age technology has made it all vastly more sophisticated, but essentially the teamwork remains the same.

Right: More than 30 years later came another day that Mauro Povia will never forget. The retired Pirelli tyre-fitter and Juan Manuel Fangio reunited in 1990 with the Alfa 159 in the hills that surround Monte Carlo.

In August 1957 Pirelli's tyre-fitter Mauro Povia played a vital part in enabling Fangio to win the world championship for a record fifth time. Practice at the old Nürburgring showed that the Pirelli 'Green Spot' tyres on which he was running had a life of only about eight laps. Fangio would therefore have to make two pit stops for tyre changes during that year's German Grand Prix, and the time lost could lose him the race.

The longer-lasting 'Red Spot' tyres would be the answer—but how to get them from Milan when almost all Italy was on holiday?

Povia heard Pirelli's executives debate this agonising question, and interrupted. 'They're already here. I thought I'd better load 40 Red Spots onto the truck before leaving Milan—just to be on the safe side. So here they are fitted, inflated and ready to race.'

Infinitely grateful and hugely relieved, his bosses almost smothered Povia in a collective embrace!

Fangio's famous race is recorded on page 53 of this book. He seized his victory by charging perilously through each corner in a higher than normal gear, and by bedding-in his new rear tyres with a vengeance—his fabulous Maserati 250F leaving the ground lap after lap as it rocketed over each crest of the undulating Nürburgring.

After congratulating Fangio on his fifth world championship, the late Mike Hawthorn said, 'If I hadn't moved over, I'm sure the old devil would have driven right over me!'

Later, Fangio was enjoying a quiet celebration with a few friends when he noticed the Pirelli team eating at a nearby table. He walked over to the group, shook Povia by the hand and thanked him for his foresight.

Recalling that meeting, Mauro Povia, who is now a pensioner living in Milan, said, 'It was one of the greatest moments of my life.'

■ ■

This account of the part played by a tyre-fitter in an historic Grand Prix is dedicated to all the behind-the-scenes unsung heroes of motor racing—past, present and future.

■ ■ ■

AN UNSUNG HERO

PIRELLI ALBUM OF MOTOR RACING HEROES

PICTURE CREDITS

Pictures, and memorabilia by kind permission of:

Allsport

A.P. Photos

Bernard Cahier

Chris Nixon

Cyril Posthumus

Dave Friedman Photographic Services

Diana Burnett

John Surtees

Ludvigsen Library, London

Martin Holmes

Mercedes-Benz Museum

Nigel Snowdon

Phil Sayer, photographer & Pavilion Books Limited

Phipps Photographic

Pirelli

Popperfoto

Quadrant Picture Library

Stirling Moss

The National Motor Museum, Beaulieu

Designed by Gill White assisted by:

Erica Hare

Trisha Isles

Seymour Quilter

Typesetting by Wyvern Typesetting

Pirelli Coordinamento Pneumatici SpA and the Derek Forsyth Partnership Limited have made every effort to contact copyright holders of the photographs reproduced in this book. If they have inadvertently failed to contact any such copyright holder they would welcome any information which would enable them to do so.